SHRED!

Running and Being

Kevin Carollo

North Dakota State University Press
Fargo, North Dakota

North Dakota State University Press
Dept. 2576, P.O. Box 6050, Fargo, ND, 58108-6050
www.ndsupress.org

SHRED! Running and Being
By Kevin Carollo

First Edition
First Printing

LCCN: 2024933559
ISBN: 978-1-946163-53-0

Cover & interior design by Nayt Rundquist

The publication of *SHRED! Running and Being* is made possible by the generous support of the Muriel and Joseph Richardson Fund and donors to the NDSU Press Fund, the NDSU Press Endowed Fund, and other contributors to NDSU Press.

This is a work of nonfiction; the author assumes responsibility for any factual errors.

Kimberly Wallin, Director
Suzzanne Kelley, Publisher
Kyle Vanderburg, Assistant Acquisitions Editor
Mike Huynh, Graduate Assistant in Publishing
Sarah W. Beck, Manuscript Intern

Printed in the USA

Publisher's Cataloging-in-Publication
(Provided by Cassidy Cataloguing Services, Inc.)

Names: Carollo, Kevin, author.
Title: Shred! : running and being / Kevin Carollo.
Description: First edition. | Fargo, North Dakota : North Dakota State University Press, [2024]
Identifiers: ISBN: 978-1-946163-53-0 (trade paperback)
Subjects: LCSH: Carollo, Kevin. | Long-distance runners--United States--Biography. | COVID-19 Pandemic, 2020---Social aspects. | Running--Social aspects. | Life. | Loss (Psychology) | Dementia. | LCGFT: Autobiographies. | BISAC: SPORTS & RECREATION / Running & Jogging. | BIOGRAPHY & AUTOBIOGRAPHY / Memoirs. | FAMILY & RELATIONSHIPS / Life Stages / Mid-Life.
Classification: LCC: GV1061.15.C37 A3 2024 | DDC: 796.42092--dc23

SHRED!

to Anne Brandt,

my reason for
writing, running,

and being. Mom,
you are the start

and finish line
of this book and

every page in
between. It all

begins with and
comes back to you,

its heartbeat.

SHRED!

February 9, 2021

I woke up this morning to Gracie, an almost eighteen-year-old cat, howling for all the things that make another morning on this devastated planet worth getting out of bed: dripping water from the shower, vigorous petting on the futon, treats scattered on the floor in front of her. Then comes more lavishing of attention, typically in multiple rooms throughout her upstairs domain. Gracie, my cakey sweets, my furry nautilus of possibility, she who has taught me so much about patience, persistence, and pacing.

Gracie will usually keep howling until I comply with her every desire, so there is little to no chance of falling back asleep. As usual, I was deep into the final episode in a series of anxiety dreams—Netflix for the unconscious—where I was having trouble getting from point A to point B. Sometimes there are other people in the dream, but they can't help me figure things out. Sometimes my surroundings seem strangely familiar and familiarly strange—a precarious mountain pass (I'm afraid of heights), a turbulent airplane (I hate to fly), a broken elevator (I'm claustrophobic), an elaborately architected and decidedly non-grid city in which I invariably get lost, a post- and/or pre-industrial wasteland with its own undisclosed codes of conduct, or a baroquely inspired and labyrinthine college campus where I'm always running behind—sometimes many hours behind—on the first day of the semester.

Gracie puts her right polydactyl paw (always the right one) on my left arm in a singular and special embrace that we share, and it is the cutest thing. I hold her as if our mutual wellbeing depends on it, as if this is the last day on Earth that we have together. I hug her in the knowledge that day is coming, I just don't know when.

Yesterday I spent all day working through a book about running and being in the end times—this book—only leaving the sunroom sofa, where I've lived for the better part of a year and counting, for a reluctant five-mile run (at 7:07 minutes per mile) in between editing rounds. I didn't really want to go outside, to be completely honest. But, given what I'm writing about, and the desire to keep my running streak since the first of the year alive, I suited up even when the phone informed me that it was -1°F, with a wind chill of -19°F, purported to be the warmest temperature of the day. If we're lucky, today will get above 0°F, but only just.

As I write, I hear Gracie again upstairs, and I have to heed her howl. She's got my number. The other cat, Woodman, is relaxing in the sink in the downstairs bathroom, gusts of heating-vent wind perhaps approximating the savannah of his dreams.

I think a lot—too much, I suspect—about the sun, winter, and weather in general. I intone my mantra—*shred*—to myself, envisioning the "e" in the middle as signifying "elemental" and "ecstatic" and "empathetic" ways of being in the world. We often refer to the weather as the elements, after all. I begin with the premise that we need to begin to truly see each other to make singular, harmonic, revelatory, ecstatic, and dynamic meaning. Read between the lines of this running log to evince other meaningful acrostics to take with us on the road to *shred*.

Running is elemental movement, a transformative force for good, a singularly meaningful practice—and survival mechanism—that compels us to move beyond the psychic barriers that define contemporary existence, a worldview predicated on division and destruction, a world seemingly all too eager to move from endangered to extinct in a single bound. Today, I invite you to become part of a movement of movement in which we move toward each other as if our very lives depend on it. I have come to believe that they do—and that our time is running out.

This movement of movement is for everyone, and that means I want to move in harmony with you at your pace. As such, pace isn't irrelevant by any stretch of the imagination, but speed is. If the idea of running seems distasteful to you, fear not. We will find a new way of moving in tandem, a singular and dynamic setting into motion that we begin together, shredding as one. Behind all the static in our lives, an ecstatic revelation about the meaning of existence awaits. Just keep moving. If, on the other hand, you find yourself wanting to go out for a run—perhaps your very first—then by all means, get after it! Then tell me all about it.

Along the way, I ruminate on poetry and language; a lifetime of teaching world literature; the '70s and '80s; the pandemic and contemporary politics; dementia; animals (human and otherwise); music; consciousness; the death of my father, Jack Ronald Carollo, in 2018; as well as manifold mother figures, including: Mother Earth; mother tongues; my partner Lonna's mom, Elizabeth Renee Gregory, who was diagnosed with early onset dementia in 2013; and of course my mom, Anne Brandt, who has been a lifelong partner-in-crime in my running journey, from before my very first marathon at age twelve, through a good quarter-century of mostly not running, to my running reboot in 2012, when I unwittingly reverted back to that shy and geeky twelve-year-old with an uncontrollable urge (cue Devo) to shred. I lovingly intersperse

a handful of verse
at various points
throughout the course

of the narrative, to serve as periodic poetic checkpoints along the way, each one acting as a kind of fueling station by the side of the narrative road.

I've structured the narrative as an old-school running log, envisioning each entry like every day and every run: as a deceptively ordinary occasion masking extraordinary insight and epiphany. In this sense, it mimics the work of Jim Fixx, whose 1977 bestseller *The Complete Book of Running* completely dates me, and whose complementary running logs first got me into recording my runs for posterity. At some point, I realized I was channeling two other books in particular: George Sheehan's *Running and Being: The Total Experience*, first published in 1978, right around the time I started playing with the idea of maybe running a 10K. There have been later editions of *Running and Being* (Sheehan passed in 1993), but such a seminal work deserves an update.

The other book is Natalie Goldberg's *Writing Down the Bones: Freeing the Writer Within*, originally published in 1986, the year I graduated high school, and right around the time I quit running competitively for a long time. At the time, I thought it was for forever, but I was wrong.

Using principles of Zen meditation practice, Goldberg's book embodies the plain and profound truth that we are all storytellers welling up with the innate desire to use language to make deep and lasting connections with one another. I still opt to teach *Writing Down the Bones* in intro to creative writing classes, even though it, too, always threatens to date me as an '80s throwback with precious little applicable computer literacy for the new millennium, someone for whom Zoom is a '70s-era show on PBS. So be it.

If anything, the pandemic has taught me a paradox of time for the end times: that the last five or so months seem to have lasted a lifetime, and simultaneously that, in the end, the last forty or so years of running and being is really no time at all.

This running log ends the way it does—that is to say, why, where, when, and how it does—for a reason. That said, the ending is also a beginning, the first step in the human race you and I already share. Another beautiful paradox that runners know all too well: the finish line is also a starting line. I'm waiting for you there, screaming myself hoarse in the final stretch, in awe of your superhuman accomplishment and your amazing grace.

But I know that this is just the warmup, and we're just stretching and shaking out the legs in nervous anticipation of what is to come. We know that making it to the starting line healthy is half the battle. We don't know the course, or what today's race truly has in store for us, but we can feel it in our bones that something elementally momentous is about to begin. I'll see you out there.

The Runner's Dream

The one where I
take the lead but
then have to aqua-
jog on air Always

waking up right
before being caught
by the pack I never
look back Always

waking up before
the alarm As if
insomnia is part
of the dream

Yesterday, i.e., 35
years later I read
a book entitled
Spirit Run Today

I went for a run
in the latest pair
of Ghosts Even
quarantine can

turn a tick other-
worldly No more
fixing run-ons or
wonky syntax I

take a page from
the marsupials' book
I want a poem that
travels at the speed

of wombat I want
a poem that dies
by running to here
from Marathon

September 8, 2020

Yesterday turned chilly, and we put the heat on for the first time. The summer ended unannounced, like so many things these days. I've now dedicated six months to quarantine, spending over 90 percent of my life in the same house, and being as vigilant as possible regarding masks, disinfectant, social distancing, and so on, despite the fact that many of my compatriots choose not to—or can't afford to—shelter in place.

So, though the malaises and uncertainties of the day are palpable, the insomnia and depression all too real, the generalized anxiety and pervasive sense of hopelessness interminable, I begin this rumination with the fledgling hope that you, beautiful stranger, will come to know that I'm on your side. I want to run and write myself into something that changes the game—our game—something that not only changes my life, but imagines a better world for us all, an alternative collective journey of radical justice. Perhaps a last-gasp effort at being at home in the world.

I know I've done things since the pandemic disrupted everything, but they seem inconsequential, unimportant. I know I feel better when I shop small, avoid Amazon, keep donating to charities—I am immensely fortunate to be able to do so—and do something other than binge-watch alternative media, *Law and Order: SVU*, and my favorite global sports: soccer, tennis, and running. And yet I've also come across some incredible music via YouTube in the process: Emily Remler's *Firefly*, Don Cherry's *Om Shanti Om*, anything and everything by Laraaji.

I have to start somewhere, and though I have a lot on my mind regarding America's "farewell tour," to paraphrase Chris Hedges's recent book—including our propensities for endless war, fossil fuel, institutionalized violence, economic disparities and despair, environmental devastation, tech addiction, and, of course, the global pandemic—I'm going to begin by considering the elemental nature of running.

Running is something I've thought a lot about over the years, and it's safe to say that, like most things, I spend way more time thinking about running than actually doing it. The same goes for writing: the previous 300-or-so words could and should have been written months ago, but now is not the time to beat myself up about it. Every word I happen to type also contains something of the elemental, linguistic cursors of a search for meaning and purpose.

The same goes for running. I try to appreciate every time I stop procrastinating and get out on the roads. I try to embrace every step and every mile as elementally good: no matter how it feels, no matter what mood I'm in, no matter how long it's been since my last outing, no matter that I have a checkered past with belief, follow-through, and joy.

I know writing can have similar stakes, that considering the confluence of form, cadence, image, words, and the world at large, can bring me back to the elemental nature of writing. It's not even a poem or an essay yet, but something elemental is accessed when I start playing with words. Poetry in motion, indeed.

If I start thinking about progress or achievement, the singular and elemental experiences of writing and running may become compromised. My self-interested desire for accolades and recognition may take over, and I start wondering why it's so hard for me to publish a damn poem once in a while. Similarly, my running mind might go off course, berate me for not being consistent with training, chastise me for squandering my youthful potential of almost forty years ago, or compare me Strava-style with others who seem infinitely more successful, driven, or serious than I've ever been, or perhaps ever will be.

> I realize these desires
> are unavoidable, part and
> parcel of the terrain of
> contemporary American life,

a culture that privileges achievement and wealth for the few rather than creating a vibrant and sustainable environment and economy for the many. Running can be articulated as an aspect of fitness, that semantic gymnasium of class and (predominantly) white privilege. But I contend that running can also be practiced alternatively—within a capitalist framework, to be sure—as collectively and spiritually transformative, with the same global and cosmic imperatives as writing.

It's like the periodic ads on YouTube interrupting a Laraaji jam, the moment when I am reminded that the mystical is couched in and shot through with the opportunistic. You can't run away from or write yourself out of capitalism. But you can run and write toward a cosmic sense of collective justice and global joy. The alternative is a profound despair, what author David Foster Wallace intimated as that eerie "sense of mostly having not done," of having lived a life of no consequence or apparent purpose.

Laraaji is chanting "I am here now" and "everything everywhere at the same time," then laughs to himself at the very thought. It makes me recall my marathoner-poet friend Fred repeating "right where we are" in the early miles of the 2013 Grandma's Marathon in Duluth, Minnesota. Just a couple times, but I've held onto those four words as an elemental mantra, an existential koan for running and being in the pandemic era. I can access the past through Fred's words, hold onto them as the most beautiful of paradoxes.

Right where we are. Welcome to the shred.

September 9, 2020

Yesterday I ran an easy 5K, about 7:06 minutes per mile, which turns out to be my typical pace, give or take twenty seconds or so per mile. I know because my lowest-of-the-low-end Garmin told me so. I bought it at Beyond Running, my go-to local store and running community that has done so much to provide a home to all wayward souls who answer the call to shred.

My partner Lonna just ordered a substantially more tricked-out Garmin from them, three-and-a-half times as much as I paid, and online it looks simultaneously elegant and legit—and utterly fitting for Lonna, who clearly needs to move on from her Fitbit. I, clearly, wear a watch that suggests "wanted to start small and see if I liked recording every mile for posterity," except I've never bothered to figure out how to upload my workouts to the computer so as to better track and potentially share my progress (or apathy) with others over the long term.

I write what the watch tells me on a membership calendar—this year's is from Amnesty International—with a pen that sits on a stack of *Runner's World* and *Running Times* magazines I'm reluctant to recycle. Every day in the running room I think about coming to the end of the age of print media, how bad my handwriting has gotten over the years, and how every day is an occasion to fight for peace and justice for all.

I'm trying to find a way to connect the myriad strands of my life mentally and elementally, and direct them towards a resonant and collective feeling of radical empathy. In this simple act, I start to create a moment of psychic interconnection between running and language, literature, the environment, and the hungry, suffering, and persecuted world in its entirety.

On a kinetic level, I don't want to lose the relationship to writing that exists in a pen on paper, or forget that there was a time when print media, like pen pals, were how we kept up with each other, and how we learned about the local and global dimensions of running at the same time.

Of course, the imagined community that political scientist Benedict Anderson saw coming into being with the spread of newspapers has now become diffuse and heterogeneous (e-journals, online databases, chat groups; Facebook, Strava, et al.; twenty-four-hour updates, bell notifications, livestreams, etc.) and his idea of a national consciousness that unifies a disparate people seems almost archaic, certainly quaint. The tricked-out watch or cellphone inevitably cedes precious headspace to the very American culture of surveillance.

Back to thinking about yesterday's run. From the watch's perspective, it has an almost laughably typical feel to it. I don't know if it's an internal sense of pacing or the unimaginative default setting of the apathetic runner, but I often seem to end up doing the same workout over and over. Maybe my internal clock is telling me to ditch the watch entirely, which I do on occasion. I like to know what the watch thinks about my workout, but I don't want the watch to insinuate that I'm somehow falling short of my goal. The goal is singularity.

On the treadmill, which I rely on during the Fargo winters (before the pandemic, at least), the same thing happens. I try to start out easy, vary the pace and distance from workout to workout, but invariably end up doing some variation of a progressive tempo run, typically starting at 7:00 flats and ramping up to sub-6:00 pace at the end of a 10K. I once ran eighteen miles at a 7:00-minute pace on a treadmill, but I don't think I'll do that ever again.

While we're on the topic: I don't listen to podcasts or music, or watch TV, on the treadmill. I don't cover the minutes and miles with a magazine—like I mentally do with the Garmin. I try to embrace each minute as it comes, until I'm forced to play mental games to see through the digital readout to the singularity of each moment, the blurry beauty of each inaudible tick of the clock, seconds joyously pacing themselves as they bleed into each other, poetry in motion. If the treadmill happens to be counting down, that's okay, too. I can mentally follow the seconds, as if peeling back time. As with the watch, I've never taken the time to figure out how to program a treadmill.

Whereas I try not to look at my watch outside—not until at least a couple miles have been recorded—or I might play mental games around how long I can go without looking at the watch on the treadmill, I commit to being hyperconscious about time, distance, pace, incline, and so on. All the while reminding myself to note the hidden singularities behind the apparent sameness of time. This works for a while, though of course I often just want to get the workout done and dusted.

There are both historical and practical reasons for me to practice awareness on the treadmill, including taking in the surroundings of everyone else at the YMCA. Namely, I have a Sicily-shaped scar on my back from falling on a treadmill when I was fourteen years old in the early '80s. The slip occurred at a doctor's house with twenty-some people watching me try out the new technology. I didn't use a treadmill for many years, and from around seventeen to my early forties I ran sporadically at best, some years not at all.

I recall logging a few miles on a treadmill in Pittsburgh over twenty years ago at my friends Jonathan and Carrie's home. That might have been my first time back. I also remember the killer guitar I bought in a pawnshop there, which has thankfully received more use on my end than anyone's treadmills.

When I came back to the running fold in 2012 in Fargo, I fell back in love with it hard, but it hasn't made me fall in love with the cold. I met people who avoided the treadmill at all costs, who ran through the ice and snow and thirty-below-not-including-wind-chill days of January and February. I have the utmost respect for these dreadmill naysayers, and on occasion I have joined them on their foolish and pointless quests to prove that the brutal, sub-zero days here are not that bad in the end, and in fact can be invigorating.

But for the most part I've decided that I require base temps in the double digits—above zero, mind you—before I'll consider going out for a run. Of course, that may change depending on the cryptic transmission vectors of the pandemic, as I'm not comfortable working out at the Y at this time (though it is indeed open).

A beautiful paradox: we can return to the singular nature of being many times over.

The s in shred
is for singularity,
step by step
starting over
over and over.

September 12, 2020

Three days ago, on Wednesday evening, I ran five miles at 6:46 pace. Then I switched to mornings and ran three miles at 7:12 pace before a chiropractic appointment. I started trying out chiropractic care last year in the hopes that I could run pain-free. Both Achilles tendons can hurt, and ever since cracking my sacrum twice six years ago, I often have significant pain in the hips during the second half of a marathon. More often than not, I'm walk-jogging the last ten miles of the 26.2. It's a conundrum I sometimes want to figure out; other times I want to move on from the allure of the marathon and the desire to push my body to its outermost limits, which of course usually means showing up for months on end, putting in the miles both patiently and intently for the duration of the training block.

As I write this, someone from the Beyond Running crew sent photos of a group of five running in the overcast, drizzly morning. I'm thinking about running, enough to start writing about it, but can't manage to be up and ready to go by 7:00 a.m. I also have only run with other people a handful of times since the pandemic gun went off, and I've refrained from any evening group gatherings. I keep distant from everybody on my solo runs, and go out of my way to give families and dog walkers a wide berth. Though Fargo feels more business-as-usual, having baseball games and yard sales without masks or social distancing, I don't want to validate the notion of runners and running as part of the problem. That said, I would like to get out there with the crew and be able to keep up.

I've stopped champing at the bit to get back to racing. It's way too soon to count on resuming regular races in 2021, and planning for them involves a curious cocktail of uncertainty, hope, and frustration. And though I ran a virtual 5K last Monday, as part of a Labor Day run sponsored by the New Orleans Track Club for Pride week, I don't really believe in the idea of virtual races. Right now, in fact, the Boston Marathon is being run virtually, but I think we can all agree that the only way to run Boston is to run the actual course from Hopkinton to Boylston Street. Talk about singularity!

And though I'd rather have run in New Orleans last weekend, the virtual 5K was perhaps a small expression of solidarity, and so I ran with NOLA and PFLAG in my heart on the gray, windy streets outside my house in Fargo. I could have called any day that weekend my 5K, really, but on Monday I donned the bib and raced myself, which I suppose is what we're doing most of the time when we race. I'm happy with the effort as a way to gauge my fitness at the end of an unmotivated summer. I guess I'm in 18:20 shape, but of course it was a rather lonely endeavor, the polar opposite of a communal, in-person event.

I didn't see the chiropractor for four and a half months, and now I've been adjusted four or five times in the last couple of months. Especially in a time of social distancing, I'm appreciative of being reminded that someone can read my body with her hands. Virtual consultation in this instance would be like a virtual Boston.

I got my teeth cleaned in late August, and as of yesterday a surprisingly quick haircut, but the chiropractor is my only semi-regular appointment. It's a masked affair, but takes place in a building that isn't always pandemic-appropriate. I try to proceed with caution and awareness, but not fear.

At all hours of the day and night, I tell myself to relax my jaw. In the parking lot, I try not to judge the mask-less tenants of the building, the mask-less janitor who always seems to be mopping in front of the chiro's office when I show up, my mask-less fellow human beings who may be forced by necessity to work in unsafe conditions, and all the mask-less, disenfranchised millions who have been failed by our government, and the mask-less, all-pervasive feeling of desperation in the air, the climate grief and the endless war and the social unrest and the racial injustice and the species extinction and on and on.

I run as if running may be a means to become whole again. I run because it may be the only time of the day where my body and mind might synch up and work together for a common purpose, for mutual enlightenment. I run in search of a collective unconscious that embraces uncertainty, intangibility, alterity. The idea of shred runs toward Singularity, Harmony, Revelation, Ecstasy, and Dynamism.

In the world of shred, then, running alone is not an option. Each run contains multitudes. Right where we are.

Yesterday, September 11, was my 52nd birthday. I ran 52 minutes at a 7:01 pace, adding one-tenth of a mile for good luck, as well as to round off the run at 7.5 miles. I may look at my watch a few more times than usual on this day, as I like to consider my life on my birthday as a kind of time-lapse run, each minute equating to a year, every moment one of potential revelation.

At around six minutes, I kicked a soccer ball from a girls' practice that had rolled into the street. Using my weaker left foot, I initially hit the curb and it bounced back to me. My second attempt was better. I hadn't touched a soccer ball in years, though I watch soccer regularly, and was excited for the English Premier League's start today. Always anticipate the rebound.

Midway through the time-lapse life-run, i.e., the mid-twenties, a man started playing "Amazing Grace" on bagpipes by Fargo's Red River. I've been thinking a lot about half my life ago—twenty-six was one of the roughest years on record for me. The words "saved a wretch like me," intoned internally, had never felt so literal.

At thirty-five minutes, I moved to Fargo–Moorhead, and so it was appropriate that I found myself by the Red River downtown, near the Radisson where I stayed for my on-campus interview at MSUM in December of 2002. I thought about living a third of my life here, the flood of 2009, getting back into running seriously—some would say obsessively—in 2012, at the age of forty-three-going-on-forty-four. I recall how long running seven miles for the first time in forever felt back then, eight years ago on more or less the same course.

There are fifty-two cards in a deck, fifty-two weeks in a year. Chance and Time running side by side. When I run, I am actively and intently making fifty-two a year of reckoning and survival. As I write this, I am thinking about how utterly fast the past fifty-two years have gone, and how my run yesterday has quickly and unassumingly become part of that past. During every run, I shall express eternal gratitude for the ephemeral and evanescent moments of harmony—in mind and body and heart and world.

September 14, 2020

Yesterday I did my pandemic strength work, just about fifteen or so minutes of planks, squats, and light barbell reps. I don't feel comfortable heading to the Y these days, although two to three times a week I was in the habit of logging a few easy miles to and from the downtown facility, and hitting a dozen machines hard, maxing out the lift with eight to twelve reps on each machine and no breaks—just as I was taught on Nautilus machines back in the '80s.

My high school friend Emery Buchner taught me how to circuit weight-train at a Nautilus facility owned and operated by his mother. I remember him taking me through the machines the first time, urging me on while stressing good form for each machine. Emery was serious about health and staying in shape; I remember when he got a tattoo of an actual nautilus on his shoulder in the late '80s. He eventually became a nurse, got married, and moved to Austin, Texas. We didn't keep in touch, although he and our friend H did.

I always assumed Emery was the happiest of our lot, the one who made the life he'd always wanted, without all the existential dread or mental breakdown that characterized me and many of my friends in the '80s. When Emery took his own life, on New Year's Eve 2017, I was so far removed from his world that I didn't get the story from H until the following summer, while I was reckoning with the loss of my father. I'm balking at using the phrase the "full story," because Emery left behind some gaping holes in his narrative. H and I had both spent time in psych wards—H in the '80s, me in the '90s—and over the years we've shared a reciprocal understanding of the fraught and often overwhelming nature of existence. I still remember anecdotes from his psych ward days, like the patient who believed a world war involving everybody against everybody else was imminent. Come to think of it, he may have been on to something there.

The first thing
someone said
to me that
first day in
a different
psych ward:
"There are
devils in the sky,

but you're not
one of those,
are you?"

Now I think about Emery every time I hit the machines at the Y—and whenever I *think* about working out at the Y, for that matter—days like today, which also happens to be H's birthday. I mentally call out to Emery, imagine that he's there spurring me on like old times. I tell him I won't give in to the pain or the fear. Some days, it is incredibly hard to make good on that promise.

The day after our twenty-year high school reunion, in 2006, Emery and I raced a lap around the high school track. I remember wearing some ridiculous sweatpants, and wasn't training at the time by any means. We'd just gone "around the lake," the two-mile warmup or cooldown that we used to do before and after intervals on the Libertyville High School track. I'm sure racing a 400m wasn't my idea. I mostly associated that track with the unappealing team workouts of quarters and halves at five-minute pace, usually multiple times a week.

Though I led comfortably for the first 200m, I knew Emery's competitive streak would take over. I believe I ended up clocking around sixty-three seconds, which now seems like some serious shredding for someone in his late thirties, especially as I spent the second half trying to hike up my damn sweatpants to get better turnover. Emery, a pole vaulter by trade and wearing shorts, dialed in a 62.

It was a sunny day; H and friend Liz were there as well. I have no lost love for the track, and it's rare and with decided reluctance that I go on one for intervals. Whenever I do, however, the endorphin rush afterwards is incredible.

I ended up not running on Saturday, but after the strength work yesterday, I ran four miles at 6:56 pace. Fargo is typically incredibly windy, so any run involves a certain amount of strength and resistance training. Though a state addicted to fracking and fossil fuels, second only to Texas in oil production, North Dakota is notoriously blustery, the proverbial poster child for investing in wind power (cue Thomas Dolby: "switch off the mind and let the heart decide").

Speaking as a runner, it's kind of a buzzkill. Unlike running at elevation, running into the wind doesn't feel like a positive way to boost one's fitness, and during a windy race I tend to be both bummed about and resigned to slower times. I don't even particularly enjoy having the wind at my back, though of course it's preferable. I remember the other Kevin from Beyond Running saying he liked the way the wind cooled him off during a half marathon a few years ago in Grand Forks, North Dakota. I've tried to adopt his attitude during this time of non-racing—seriously, it's been noticeably windy on every damn run of the last six months—and appreciate the minutes where I'm not constantly brushing the bangs out of my face and mouth.

The wind is not my friend. But I'll allow that there is something ethereal and eerie about its omnipresence here. To get to shred's "r" of revelation, one must run through the "r" of reckoning. I go outside with the belief that the phantom presences of Emery and my father and so many others will swirl around me, borne on a wind as unrelenting as my yearning.

September 16, 2020

After a couple of weeks back to regular, consistent running, I fell off the shredwagon for a couple of days. Almost immediately, I began despairing. Indeed, there is much to despair about these days. I watched *Democracy Now!* and went straight to lamenting the loss of millions of acres of forest, the breaking off of an iceberg twice the size of Manhattan, never to return, the increasing death tolls and infection rates across the globe, the burning of the Amazon, as devastating to biodiversity and cultural survival as the recent fires in Australia, and an American economy addicted like North Dakota to fracking and fossil fuels. All the while those in power seem uninterested in saving the planet, or helping out the disenfranchised working class, or putting the brakes on the forever war machine.

Part of me has stopped believing in a better future. Everything on the macro-level points to mass extinction, great unrest with no subsequent revolution in consciousness, and the death of the humanities presaging the death of humanity. What does one study in the university of the apocalypse if not the schizophrenic contours of an apoplectic universe?

If I'm not careful, my mind will run away from me. I envy the people who wake up with a sense of purpose or feeling of certainty about their place in the world. I see runners who are more committed to and serious about their training, as well as others from all walks of life who seem less hampered by the fear and loathing that routinely debilitate me. Just as I think about running way more than I actually run, I think about writing way more than I actually write, and I deftly and easily convince myself that this is somehow wrong, akin to ill-advisedly using too many adverbs. I can unconsciously fall into the trap of looking at the success of my peers—my faster, better-published, more dedicated and accomplished friends—and feel that I've somehow once again fallen short, and that I've squandered a fair amount of potential and privilege along the way to boot. Thinking about me and only me, however, is like living in a padded cell.

For the record, I rather dig adverbs, and so shall use them brashly and unashamedly henceforth.

I also keep myself from acknowledging anything I *do* accomplish, or from relishing any chance achievement that came with putting myself out there, by regularly "showing up," to paraphrase

American marathoner and 2018 Boston champion Des Linden. By now, I know that the solution is as simple and elemental as a mantra. I have to put one recalcitrant foot in front of the other until I remember—elementally, intuitively, naturally, viscerally—why I run, why I need body and mind to synch up in a moment of ecstatic singularity, of elemental movement. I have to start playing with words to remind myself of the possibilities of language to provide insight despite—or because of—an apparent meaningless and devastated world.

Sometimes I can manage to cough up a decent poem about the universe, without sounding overly overwrought or self-absorbed. I think of Anne Sexton's poem "Live" and the call to honor the "excitable gift," i.e., approaching language the way a litter of puppies approaches life. Unbridled curiosity, untamable reverence. I ritually forget this intense feeling of dynamic intent, often going months without writing a poem, or getting excited about the gift of language itself, for that matter. I might become overly concerned with publishing something, errantly following the "greedy soul" that Robert Bly talks about. As if a poem needs a name in print to be legit.

I've also become expert at overthinking the run. Deep down, I know I'm meant to do it—others would say I have the body for it—and it only takes a couple of miles to remind body and mind of this fact. Like Anne Sexton, Steve Prefontaine famously spoke of "the gift," and how to give anything less than your best was to forsake it. The good news is that we all have it; the excitable gifts of language and motion are for all. Really, any words, any pace, will do just fine. We are just warming up to the idea of ecstasy, which is ultimately and elementally the sensation of being outside oneself, *ek-stasis*, no stasis—but movement, energy, change, transformation.

Even so, I got up this morning completely bitchy and irritable. I woke up having forgotten the most basic elements of existence.

I had to relearn
all the lessons
of the last six
months all over
again. My ego
stood in the way
of revelation
and survival.

In running lay the possibility of stepping outside of my default setting, which is to be an ego-driver on a crash course with pointlessness and futility. Not running can be exhausting at times, in myriad ways, as if not expending energy on a regular basis involves a kind of cumulative energy depletion.

I started with the strength exercises, not even sure if I'd make it outside afterwards. I often tell myself that the strength training can be enough for a day, just fifteen or so minutes where I feel the burn of a plank or a rep, and then I can go back to watching tennis clips and animal rescue videos until I feel existentially numb again. Then I made pizza dough, which has become quite therapeutic during the pandemic. Then I told myself that I could run for five minutes and twenty seconds and be done with it or extend that to two or three miles if I felt like it, no big deal. The main element in my existential training regimen is to keep showing up; distance or time is irrelevant.

Obviously, this sounds somewhat counterintuitive to the competitive runner, who tracks progress by regular workouts and weekly mileage tallies, investing several months of a training cycle toward an end goal and level of fitness. And by the time I'm two miles into a run, I often start to feel like there's no reason not to keep going, at least for another mile or two, just to say I did.

I ended up running 5.25 miles at a 6:49 pace, the legs feeling solid after a couple days off. See what I did there? I took my overwhelming anomie and turned it into two reset rest days. Everything felt good, natural, meant to be. At around mile two, I ran across a park with a couple of dogs off their leashes. I watched the smaller of the two, Mimi, chase me down from a hundred yards away, a dog who wanted nothing more than to run around me while nipping at my heels. Running is simply an elemental and beautiful game for most of us.

My default setting is to be annoyed at having to adjust my pace to accommodate some stranger's best friend, my scowl for a dog's smile. I slowed to a trot in an attempt to sheepdog a dog back to her human. It took several tries, as each time I started picking up the pace, Mimi believed it to be game on. Her human apologized to me, but by then I kind of wanted to keep playing this running game with Mimi. Almost as if I was someone else, I told Mimi's human that there were no worries, that we were all out here having fun. And I truly meant it.

September 18, 2020

I often start the morning in a foreign language. This morning I read a couple poems in Spanish by the Peruvian poet Mónica Belevan: *Y el sol es mi ojo, cerrado*. I can't always pretend to understand much of what I read, but as with reading poetry in any language, meaning comes secondary to enlightenment or ecstasy—concepts that may be causally connected, I'm not sure. Reading in a foreign language can incite an elemental return to "original singularity," that primal moment where one recognizes—no, one instinctively *feels*—the concentrated and talismanic energy that propels all language. Any word is the end result of a long conversation between primal gibberish and cosmic longing. Or, as Duncan Trussell and the Buddhists might say, confusion is a condition of enlightenment.

Perhaps this is why sound poetry is often so epic to me. All of one's emotions are accessible, potential and potent, words beautifully devolving to their origins, snippets of understandable discourse dissolving in a maelstrom of oceanic sound. As with Laraaji in the middle of a mystic jam, sound poetry often provokes laughter, a most wonderful and appropriate response to the absurdity of the universe.

And the sun is my eye, closed. I may think about this line all day, such that it becomes a mantra for shredding today's run, or I might file it away for future reference, as a reminder that I should get more serious about learning Spanish; or I might forget it entirely, as I forget most everything I read—indeed, as I forget most everything that happens on any given day.

But I will remember how this particular line from a longish poem does the work of poetry, in that these few words make an epic and ephemeral connection between macro and micro, the sun and the poet. What is my eye/the sun not seeing? Can an overcast day be a form of meditation, a turning inward of both individual and cosmic force? Adapting Michel de Montaigne, I might assert that my sun and eye go hand in hand.

Because I speak French way better than Spanish, perhaps, my eye initially translated "sol" as "soil" or earth. *The earth is my eye, closed*. I quite like that mistranslation as well. I only plan to run a few miles today, but I'm ready to groove on this connection between earth, eye, and sky.

Meanwhile, in
the sunroom

the morning
sun is an eye
opening and
closing, making
googly eyes
with the earth.

Yesterday I ran five miles at a 6:37 pace, so I know it's fall. I'd intended on running at least twenty or so seconds per mile slower, but without looking at my watch until the last quarter mile, I ended up running faster than the day before, with seemingly the same or less effort. Fall is that sweet spot for Fargo running, and some years autumn only seems to last a few weeks. The winters are long and harsh, as everyone knows, but summers are typically hot, humid, and windy. No one knows what spring is like, unless you mention flood season and then we kinda sorta see what you mean.

Obviously, it's cliché to joke about the weather around here, but it's also undeniable that you don't move to Fargo to enjoy it. You can embrace the terrifying beauty of thirty below, but you can't trust your running friends who ski when they say it's so great to be out in it. And to feel sweated out by 7 a.m. in the summer, or to cut workouts short because it's just too damn hot, perennially reminds me that the warm days I longed for mere weeks ago are going to discourage me from running just as much as the sub-zero wind tunnel days of November, December, January, February, March . . . then maybe a flood, with snow possible until late April, or in 2020's case, a pandemic! If I ever make a sequel to the movie *Fargo*, I'll set it during a heatwave, air-conditioning wall units dripping in back alleys, the wooden eyes of the woodchip statue of Marge, closed. Then, by the murky shores of the Red River, a body, naked . . .

In all honesty, much stranger and more macabre murders have occurred here than I could possibly make up. In fact, I live right across the street from a house where a gruesome murder took place in 2015. Now that house is a parking lot. The harsh reality of the area, often belied by notions of "Minnesota Nice" and "How Fargo of You!", involves more than the weather, and informs how I struggle to reckon with—and get right with—my immediate surroundings.

And to be completely frank, the scenery leaves a lot to be desired, but at least Fargo–Moorhead has a natural body of water between it, which is more than I can say for Champaign–Urbana, Illinois, or Phoenix-Tempe, Arizona, two other hyphenated places

I've lived (1992–2001). One comes to have an affinity for seemingly random yet very specific short stretches of residential road, or the trails along the river, or a regular route that one shares with others. I'm reminded of a slight downhill I used to run in eighth grade in Libertyville, Illinois, by Butterfield Middle School and maybe seven miles in to a ten-mile course.

It was Dan Dwyer, a runner who'd recently moved into our apartment complex right across from the high school track, and who would win some local 10Ks at the time, who first noticed how I'd unconsciously speed up turning the corner onto Butterfield, and who first dubbed it my "stretch." Dan seemed way older than I was, a real adult and all, and I no doubt wanted to impress him on our first ten-mile runs together. I was showing him my route, after all, but he probably wasn't much older than thirty at the time. To this day, I honor Dan's idea of a personal stretch, and think about how beautiful it is that, when it comes down to it, like the iconic stretch in Eugene, Oregon, we all have a Pre's Trail. I hope to extend my stretch of road beyond its unassuming beginnings, until it one day meets up with yours.

The pandemic has made running with others and my regular routes unfamiliar in some vital, compelling ways. My typical autumnal longing to shred a marathon has been diverted—perhaps I should say "postponed" or "canceled"—in favor of a different kind of training regimen. I could call it running as elemental reckoning, or how to become a shredding being, if I were interested in naming or delimiting phenomena. I'm making it up as I go along, but I go forth in the certainty that

> I've been preparing
> for this particular stretch
> my whole life.
> It is everything,
> a closed eye,
> suddenly opening.

American Unction

America was now a country
with a question mark
—Todd Gitlin

And I, too, was the uncurled fetus
of a question in the war between
now and forever. I waited a half

century in the interrogation room
of the American Dream to unlearn
how to un-ask the universe for help.

And when my father finally outlived
his unsung life, I became a question
mark keeping the door to our mutual

future ajar. Then the un-laws from
the Philippines came to the shores
of my grief to tell me how they under-

stood the difference between sapling
and tree. In Wilma's random ululations
I startled to un-hear his voice. Under-

neath it all, a telling unknowing and
every memory unraveling. I was an
unborn fetus of faith, unquestioning.

September 22, 2020

The last three days have been perfect for running, but I've stayed inside instead, except for a proverbial beer run to Fargo Brewing Company a half mile away. I do like to reward a good workout with a few beers, and fall weather and races seem to go hand in hand with the suds of Oktoberfest. Just another day in the life thinking about running more than actually doing it, just to complement thinking about writing more than actually putting the computer on my lap in the pandemic bunker sunroom and seeing where my typing hands will take me. Thus defines the predicament of the middle-aged runner and writer: constant thinking about slowing down, tiring, retiring, hanging things up, giving it all a rest.

> Not doing. Being
> okay with. And
> then what?
> Perhaps a kind
> of waiting with-
> out longing. And
> for how long?

I'm also thinking a lot about being okay with sporadic training, with keeping my finger on the pulse of the cosmic heartbeat that is actual running, even if it feels like I'm winning the virtual slack-a-thon that is 2020. These are times when committing to running a couple miles a day comes in handy, as I finally decided to do in August of 2018. I made it to two-thirds of a year, and then one day just decided to break the streak. I don't regret it. Not usually, at any rate.

I needed to commit to some kind of daily running ritual, because the longing just wasn't there. I was grieving the loss of my father, helping his widow, Wilma, in Illinois, and trying to keep it together. I occasionally tried to write poems while Wilma slept, watched the World Cup, and otherwise haunted the Chicagoland Tri-State area where I grew up. I drove my dad's car home along the Mississippi, wore his Vietnam-era army jacket into a bar in La Crosse, Wisconsin, and had a Toppling Goliath or two with a bump of single malt. In what now seems like a bizarre turn of events—as well as a long, long time ago in a galaxy far, far away—I got super high with comedian friend Adam before he opened up for Todd Glass in Minneapolis. I was burning out on all cylinders, and no doubt looked the part of a bedraggled veteran in the unwinnable war against mortality. While I was visiting Mom in Michigan, Lonna had to put down our cat Hero, Gracie's sister, on August 1.

I went on one run at Wilma's, a hot five-mile sweat-fest in July that felt good once done, but incredibly long and humbling in the doing. In June of 2016, while training for a return to Grandma's Marathon, I hit the trail behind friend Michael's sister's place in Red Wing, Minnesota, and ended up running a 10K in thirty-eight minutes and change like it was no big deal. I felt dialed in, ready to shred. A couple years later and it seemed like back to square one, more or less where I am today, a couple years on from *that* summer of reckoning, now over fifty and still trying to find my way, still trying to figure out what the fuck it all means.

Incidentally, Grandma's 2016 turned out to be extremely hot, and I brazenly went out way too fast—just over 1:20 at the half, as if I was intending to PR or something—and I fell apart in classic Carollo fashion, taking over two hours to complete the second half. Because of injury, this was my first marathon since Boston 2014, which I'd run in the now-unbelievable time of 2:44:49.

In Duluth, I was running to honor my friend Ashley's father, Butch Middleton, an army dentist who died in Germany but used to love to run Grandma's when in the States. To get to the finish line, I kept calling to him: come on Butch, let's go, as a way to get to the finish line. There is a classic photo of Butch finishing a marathon with bloody nipples, the classic running battle wound one wants to turn away from but can't stop staring at.

The 2014 Boston Marathon immediately springs to mind as a moment of great collective reckoning. I was arguably in the best shape of my life, although I'd sprained an ankle the day before the Merge Records 25K in North Carolina a month before and had to sit it out. A mere few months later—on August 27, 2014, to be precise—I would crack my sacrum and would be off running for several months. But Boston 2014 remains a quintessential moment of shred, when the myriad powers within us aligned, and the collective energy of ecstatic reckoning synched up to create a moment of dynamic and harmonious intersubjectivity. The tagline "Boston Runs as One" felt viscerally, movingly true.

Jump back two more years from Boston 2014 to the summer of 2012, and I am running my first real race in the twenty-first century, a Pride 5K in town that turned out to be around a half-mile short. I reflect on the dynamic connection between this unassuming YMCA-sponsored event and Boston, and how that year and a half would change my life forever. I didn't know it at the time, but I was returning to competing seriously—intuitively, longingly, obsessively (to paraphrase poet Deb Marquart, everything's an adverb)—for the first time since the age of sixteen. I was a month or two away from turning forty-four.

Lonna brought her mom to watch. At sixty-eight, Beth is currently in the late stages of early onset dementia. We had some suspicions in 2012, and Beth had undergone some neurological testing by then, but her world and ours wouldn't be turned upside down until May of 2013, when Beth was sixty-one and had to retire from thirty-eight years as a daycare provider in the space of an afternoon. By then, I had rejoined the running community full throttle, had run the Maratona di Roma in Italy, and was gearing up to run Grandma's for the first time the following month. A week after crying in front of the TV watching footage of the Boston 2013 bombings, I ran a half marathon in St. Cloud, Minnesota, before which we honored the victims with a reverent and moving moment of silence. It wouldn't be the last.

Running involves multiple layers of meaning, myriad palimpsests of reckoning. I run with Pride and Boston in my heart, with Butch and my father, with my mom and Beth—and with George Floyd, Breonna Taylor, and Ahmaud Arbery. I can't claim that running is the answer to how to deal with the concomitant urgencies of climate, racial, and social justice, or to the ongoing psychic tolls of dementia, intolerance, and extinction. But it is how I choose to pose the question, how I ask the universe where I should go, how I open myself up to the present moment, and—however fleetingly, tentatively, or reluctantly—glimpse a way to move forward.

Word by word, step by step, I am returning to the elemental fold of humanity, a moving tribute to all who came before me, all who come after.

September 25, 2020

Just when I think I have body and mind committed to running through the pandemic, I take some days off and have to cajole myself into doing what we were all born to do: move through this beautiful and devastated world, taking bodily and mental notes. Mindful running involves so much more than listening to one's body, as the late physician and running guru George Sheehan advised, although the body is often where reflection on running starts. At some point, we learn *not* to listen to it—or worse, come to hate it—such that the one vessel we've been given becomes a curious adversary.

When I start back up again, this time after three days off, I find that I haven't given too much up in terms of fitness. I run four miles at a 6:37 pace, the exact same pace as a five-mile run the week before. The next day I run five miles at 6:48 pace, similar to two runs last week at 6:49 pace. I'm not obsessively checking my watch in order to perform this mundane feat. Instead, I mildly marvel at how my body seems compelled to keep returning to the same pace. I always try to start out slow, but fall weather often ends up encouraging me to drop one or two sub-6:30s by the end of the run.

In the three marathons that I've run since turning fifty, I've gone through the half around 1:25 and change, really without looking at my watch. I broke three hours the first time—surprisingly with only six weeks buildup to the race (Chicago 2018). The next two were second-half nightmares (Boston 2019, Twin Cities 2019), similar to Grandma's 2016, even though I showed up to the starting line in significantly better shape both times. Now that actual marathons are cancelled for the foreseeable future—and, I suppose, a reluctance to compromise my immune system with full-on serious marathon training—I'm interested in reevaluating what running ultimately means for me. I want to find a way to better listen to the world around my body.

Aside from some basic strength work in the morning—my humble surrogate for actually hitting a dozen machines at the Y—I took yesterday off exercise. I did, however, go to see my chiropractor, which always makes me feel better in terms of energy and outlook. Though I haven't gotten a massage in several years—before because of laziness, and now because of the pandemic—I have the utmost respect and appreciation for body therapists like Dr. Kraft, who are so adept at reading the body.

After more than four months off from sharing anyone's personal space, seeing a chiropractor two or three times a month feels like a vital indulgence. I want independent practitioners like Dr. Kraft to survive the pandemic, just as I order books from Zandbroz Variety downtown, or Small Press Distribution and Powell's online, deliberately avoiding Amazon and Jeff Bezos's pandemic profiteering in order to invest instead in Main Street and the ninety-nine percent. I dare say that American freedom—or just freedom writ small—can only be truly felt when we disconnect from our disembodying devices and embrace the small—or fledgling, or humble, or tenuous, or fleeting—instances of human interaction as imminently revelatory, as inherently revolutionary. I am reminded of Jim Moore's small poem "Against Empire," the last line of which is "we are small, small lives."

Of course, I relish the regular reading of my body, with my spine as narrator of my life. Dr. Kraft takes her time with each client, going above and beyond the quick adjustment, and into the psychic and somatic realm of the "hero with a thousand faces" that is our bodies. Most clients do not see her for running-related reasons, and perhaps I have ultimately sought out chiropractic care for a deeper, more elemental reason: to share the holy scripture of my one and only body with someone who loves a good read.

I don't know how many miles I'm going to run today, or if I'll find an excuse not to go out, as if writing about running might be an adequate substitute for the practice itself. But I commit to looking up from my knees and foot strike more often than I did two days ago. I commit to small-minded and consequential running, to running against empire.

October 1, 2020

A chilly and gray morning here in Fargo, noisy construction across the street, and ambient musical genius Brian Eno on the TV. After my last entry, I stopped running for four days. The first day was intentional, in that I'd planned to do my usual strength workout, see the chiropractor, and call it good. Then the day off turned into two, then three, then four. Yet again, I thought about running every day, then at some point made a conscious decision to not run. Running is not a chore I have to get done, I told myself; it is no big deal to take a day or two off, and in fact I can benefit from taking a break, even if I'm only going out for the usual three to five miles.

Or so I tried to tell myself. Runner's guilt set in anyway, as did my body into the couch. I watched soccer on the computer, *Law and Order: SVU* on TV, tennis clips and alternative media on YouTube, like I always do. And both my body and mind responded. One doesn't exactly marvel at how quickly and easily a body and mind lapse into providing a lap for a cat, the body merely a stiff and achy vessel for the unrelenting thoughts that keep me up at night.

> In some subtle-
> yet-willful way,
> I return to
> the scrolling,
> clicking, glossing,
> and fretting me
> who is channeling
> a world in real-
> time decline.

I might get more reading done as well, I tell myself. And since the pandemic I've taken to making pizza dough every week, at least once, with homemade pizza being served at least twice a week, sometimes more. I've already mentioned a penchant for beer, and I have many beer coasters from around the world to prove it. Looking beside me in the sunroom, I'm struck with how fortunate I've been to travel over the years, as well as reminded that I can't go to any of these places, at least for the time being. No slice in New York City or pizza margherita in Napoli, and no draft at Ma Che Siete Venuti a Fà in Rome or The Livery in Benton Harbor, my local when I'm visiting Mom in Michigan. No visiting Mom, either, of course.

I look at these coasters and return to different moments of my life: Bath Ales, when I snuck away from the group for a couple pints in England in 2012. This particular coaster has a rabbit on it, and ever since reading *Watership Down* at a tender and impressionable young age (fifth or sixth grade?) I've been fascinated by rabbits. I'm on their side in the end, and I'm also on the side of the tortoise. Both go at their own pace, and both continue to carve out an existence in the Anthropocene despite the incursions of human beings making their world fraught and uncertain. All hail the tortoise and the hare!

And that's not even the half of it with this one coaster when I consider this trip to Bath occurred around the time that I was considering getting back into running hard-core. I didn't know it then, but looking back, there were some indications. I'd gone to Blackwell's in Oxford to pick up the recently released book by Adharanand Finn, *Running with the Kenyans*. I'd been getting up for short runs on the trails and in the parks surrounding Wycliffe Hall, iconic mist included with every morning. I was finding my way back to an elemental kind of shredding, but I didn't know it yet, and I was hesitant to make a big deal out of it, to consciously affirm that I wanted to run and run and run, to return to my childhood obsession with the same intent and intensity.

I also have one of many Junkyard Brewing Company coasters on the end table to my left. I remember winning the Junkyard 5K in 2017, but mostly I miss the regularity of seeing the punters at the pub. Then there's the Longman & Eagle coaster from Logan Square in Chicago, a Bir & Fud coaster from Trastevere in Rome—which reminds me of running the Rome Marathon in March of 2013, my first marathon in over thirty years—as well as a Bull City Burger and Brewery coaster from 2014, when I flew to Durham, North Carolina, to run a 25K for Merge Records's 25th anniversary a month before the 2014 Boston Marathon. As mentioned, I ended up twisting my ankle during the shakeout run the day before, pretty much a minute in, and had to bail on the race. I can't tell you how disappointed I was, drinking beer *Roadhouse Blues*-style in the hotel and reading student response papers instead of doing what I'd come to do.

In front of me, there is a coaster from The Vierling Restaurant in Marquette, Michigan, where I had the most incredible fish sandwich a few years ago. And one from the Laughing Sun Brewing Company in Bismarck, North Dakota, to remind me of my friend and fellow

Chelsea supporter Michael, as well as the running scene two hours and forty minutes due west of me, where the land gets hillier as it starts to approach the oil patch in the western part of the state.

It always takes two hours and forty minutes to drive to Bismarck from Fargo, which happens to be the time for the marathon I wanted to break in my forties. It didn't happen, and seven years after running 2:43:42 at the Twin Cities Marathon in Minnesota, it seems unlikely that I'll make a serious attempt at 2:40 in my fifties. But you never know. A basic tenet of shred is to be open to possibility, to look—yea, to *move*—beyond the sedentary and self-deprecating mind. I tell myself that the limits are unknown, that I don't know better what I am capable of, and that embracing that unknowing gives singular meaning and purpose to existence. Every day I harness body and mind to move beyond the everyday.

Both tortoise and hare are shredders. The ethos of shred has no prescribed minutes per mile. We do it together at our own pace.

Certainly, one can and should play the coaster palimpsest game with books or running bibs. The objects we surround ourselves with have a talismanic quality within them. Everything that appears mundane on the surface contains a sacred and sustaining singularity. I want to tap into that deep well of emotion and thought to get to the subjective palimpsests within the objects I've collected along the way.

Though my present training illustrates how it is all too easy to not run for yet another day, this, too, brings me back to a singular kind of muscle memory, namely two years ago when my father passed away. My father, who in 2016 told me that even God didn't want me running anymore, spent many years of his life struggling against his body, such that the idea of going for a walk around the block became distasteful. By 2016, just getting in and out of the car had become a painful ordeal for Dad. It had indeed been painful for many years, and this from an avid collector (read: hoarder) who maintained a childlike enthusiasm for life, especially books, until the bitter end.

As a teenager, I might have been running away from my father, but today I feel myself running toward him—this despite his admonition to stop running because I might hurt myself again. At the time, I asked Dad what God's opinion on me playing tennis was.

During that conversation, Dad eventually relented enough to allow that maybe I could run a 5K without too much risk. I remember meeting him and Wilma in Chicago a couple years earlier for lunch, the day after I'd won the PAWS 8K in 26:08. I thought maybe the course had been short for me to post such a fast time, but nevertheless I was on cloud nine, not so different from that fourteen-year-old winning a two-mile cross-country race. Dad's cataracts were so bad that he couldn't really see the 1st Place inscription on my medal, which I'd brought to show him. Heck, I won 200 dollars as well, so lunch was going to be on me!

By then, Dad was having trouble getting in and out of taxis, his knees making a one-block walk an epic trek. I hadn't lived with him since my parents separated in 1976, a few years before the running began in earnest the first time. Dad didn't get the poetry, either, but believed in me as a writer anyway.

Now, in the orange bedroom upstairs, I lie down next to a photo of him and me from the previous millennium, some Christmas visit in Chicago before he and Wilma moved to the 'burbs. I am surrounded by the books he gave to me: Steinbeck, Updike, Roth, and some beloved science fiction titles, as well as a couple pencil drawings he did way back when. One of a bulldog, the other of a horse.

I carry these memories of Dad with me on the run, and I pour my love and grief into the poems. I say "Hey, Dad" when I see him smiling in the photo. Then I open up a book. Just a few pages, maybe a few kilometers the following day. I hope that he would approve.

Because it's already the first of the month, I want to write a little bit longer to assess where I'm at in my thinking and training. After the aforementioned four days off, I rounded out the month of September with three miles, five miles, and four miles, all at sub-7:00 pace. Just as it is easy to fall off the shredwagon, getting back on is as simple as going out for a couple miles. I haven't lost an edge that I'm trying to sharpen, and getting after it feels more than right for right now. My mood elevates and sense of purpose returns almost immediately, estranged body and mind back in conversation with each other.

I look at the previous two months of the Amnesty calendar upstairs and note a modest increase in consistency. I proceed knowing full well my running mates are putting in the serious miles, while I'll take a couple hours to write about a half-hour run I did the other day. Eventually, I want to be able to keep up with them when they do long runs, but for now I move forward in the knowledge that I have all the time in the world to increase the mileage and intensity. Now is the time to be consistent and concerted in my thinking and training. I move at pandemic pace through the fragile and uncertain world, and I practice being open to radical transformation on even the most mundane day, the most basic workout. After all, the half hour I spend running may indeed be the only time I leave the house.

I ran seventeen days out of thirty-one in August, and twenty-one days out of thirty in September. This month I'll aim for twenty-four days, and perhaps run ten miles one day to re-demystify the idea of running longer distances. I only started writing about running three days shy of my 52nd birthday, just over three weeks ago, and am now approaching 10,000 words, proving to me that I haven't been completely idle of late. With conscious effort, but without overthinking, I'm building up a kind of consistency in body and mind, one that keeps moving toward the Singular, Harmonious, Revelatory, Elemental-ecstatic, and Dynamic nature of SHRED. My running goals have shifted from training for a specific race or PR attempt. Shredding isn't virtual, but actual, a practice that aims for a moment of dynamic, interconnected presence. I hope to learn why you run, what you dream about, and maybe run and dream together for a few miles. You choose the pace and the course.

October 6, 2020

Last week things started to fall into place. I ran every day and finished the week with thirty miles. Friday, Saturday, and Sunday were typical windy autumn days, and I ran four or five miles each day, bemused by the fact that my pace was 6:46 each day. Each day I didn't look at my watch until the final stretch, but instead told myself to just relax and soak up the cool temps outside. I reminded myself to remain mindful of the singularity of every run, each one a ritual shred done with no end goal in sight, shredding being a singular dynamic practice in and of itself. It is the goal.

That said, I almost registered for the Houston half marathon in January last week, then learned today that they're going virtual, which was to be expected. I have friends in Houston and know that vlogger Seth James DeMoor planned to run the Houston half as well. I figured that taking a trip to visit friends and run alongside 20,000 living, breathing human beings would prove to be a pipe dream, that the curve ball of 2020 wouldn't just end because the calendar says so, but it's also important to dream while we wait to meet up on course.

I'm expecting the same will hold true for all races next year, at least until the summer. I might register for Grandma's Marathon in June now, but as important as it is to have something to look forward to and prepare for in this life, it is disappointing to ritually and repeatedly gear up for a race that never happens. I deferred my registration this year for the Bix 7 race in Davenport, Iowa, so maybe by the end of July 2021 the idea of 10,000 runners lining up to run such a crazy, classic, iconic race as the Bix won't seem preposterous. I'm only being realistic when I say "ten months away!" that I'm not holding my breath.

Yesterday, Monday, I did my strength exercises and went out for an easy four-mile run. Temps had climbed back into the 70s, not unheard-of in Fargo in October, but also not typical. Again, I told myself to just relax—so much nebulous ubiquitous anxiety these days—and enjoy my only half hour in the great outdoors. Again, I didn't look at my watch until the final stretch. Guess what my pace was? Close! 6:45.

I know you're supposed to vary your workouts for many reasons, but this feels less like a rut and more like a groove. It may look the same on paper or on the watch, but of course it's not. I let the wind dictate the pace, to the point that I contemplate it as a kind of invisible training partner—ghost as guide. The wind is not my friend, but maybe it can become a frenemy.

There were many upsets this past weekend in the world of sports, from Roland Garros to Premier League soccer. Most notably, the greatest marathoner of all time and world record holder, Eliud Kipchoge, took eighth place in the elite-only London Marathon, his first loss in six years. I wonder what it's like to have an off day and still run under 2:07 for the distance.

It is fair to say that of the fifteen or so marathons I've run—I always have to recount them, then add the three I ran as a twelve-year-old—most if not all of them didn't go as planned, and the majority were out-and-out train wrecks. The two I ran in 2019—Boston and Twin Cities—were both second-half nightmares. I barely look at my watch during a marathon, and sometimes even prefer to run without one, and still manage to go through the half in 1:25 and change. Both of last year's marathons took me well over three and a half hours, and I crossed the finish line more confused and crestfallen than anything. Why does this always happen, especially when an off day should still put me close to, if not under, three hours? And why do I have mostly off days when it comes to this most epic and ecstatic of distances?

During these train wrecks, I meet up with fellow shredders who are similarly bonking, and we help each other get to the finish line. It doesn't matter if the wheels come off at mile fourteen, seventeen, or twenty-two, or, like Boston last year, when I felt pretty much finished by mile eleven, there is someone on course having the day you're having. Today I pay homage those comrades, to let you all know that I have kept meeting you on course in my heart, and that our bonking bond is for life. We'll shred the next one.

October 8, 2020

We interrupt this livestream to report that guitar legend Eddie Van Halen has left the building. After roughly reaching the halfway point in my writing workout a couple days ago, I put down the computer to watch the tear-filled reminiscences of guitarists from my generation and older who were understandably and utterly devastated by the news: EVH is dead at sixty-five.

The singer Johnny Nash, known for his 1972 hit "I Can See Clearly Now," also died on October 6 at the age of eighty. Clearly of my dad's generation, Nash's passing brings to mind all the crooners Dad used to listen to in the '70s: Johnny Mathis, Shirley Bassey, Barry Manilow. This is perhaps not the place for a rumination on the intricate and beautiful mixed-race and gender-troubling legacies of the American songbook—even Eddie Van Halen's mom is Indonesian—but it without a doubt forms and informs the musical landscape when I first laced up a pair of running shoes and slogged through that 10K sponsored by my mom's employer at the time, Condell Memorial Hospital. I barely remember running the Condell Distance Classic that first time, but I think I was eleven years old, maybe ten.

Don't bother trying to find CMH on the map, as it turned into the Medical Center of Lake County in the '80s, and perhaps still is today. If there were any races being held, I'd make a point of running one back in the town where it all started: Libertyville, Illinois.

My father, Jack Ronald Carollo, age seventy-six, died on the day Anthony Bourdain took his own life in the south of France at age sixty-one. I happened to be in Siracusa, Sicily, at the time. Anthony Bourdain seemed to live a dream life, the kind of life people who love food, wine, and travel would kill for, and to throw it all away when you're on the top of your game feels more than tragic.

I had *Van Halen I* on cassette—again, probably ten or eleven years old—and I can remember going to the record store to buy LPs and cassettes with the same obsessive passion as I hit up the running store for the latest footwear. Looking back, this ferment of music and sports came from the confusion and uncertainty surrounding my parents' separation in 1976 and eventual divorce in 1977. My stepfather, Jeff Wolf, came into the picture, and it is at that point that I became interested in playing competitive sports like soccer and baseball, as well as learning about different kinds of music. To my untrained eyes and ears, Jeff's LP collection seemed way more eclectic than Dad's—The Kingston Trio and Rush's *All the World's a Stage*—while my younger brother put on Jeff's copy of The Stylistics on the regular chez Brandt-Wolf-Carollo. Make up to break up, that's all we do.

Jeff also had an acoustic guitar lying around, and sometimes he'd strum a few chords, maybe sing "Michael Row the Boat Ashore" or "Tom Dooley." It all sounds so stereotypically '70s to me now. Moving from Palatine to Libertyville to start seventh grade in 1980 seemed to nudge me closer to trying my hands at taming Jeff's acoustic beast. With the action of its fretboard set impossibly high, I had little hope of mastering Fleetwood Mac's "Landslide" to impress the girls at the high school talent show. But it set the stage for a lifelong passion for the guitar and music, and for the moment it seemed unnecessary to choose between them and athletics. That would come during junior year of high school. For the moment, I could be the rock star training for the Olympics.

I was nowhere near to shredding on that guitar—indeed, it shredded my fingers before my fingers built up the calluses to take it—but the shred seed had been planted, albeit unbeknownst to me at the time. Forty years later, I access the inchoate curiosity of a shy child who reacted to his parents' divorce by wanting to be a part of something greater, something meaningful, something epic and triumphant. And to realize that, even then, my dreams were ultimately not about fame or success, but rather about acceptance and transformation—and deep, deep reckoning—intimates to me something invaluable about the nature of shredding, where it comes from, when it becomes manifest, and how it might work its magic today.

My stepfather passed during the summer of 2007, my father in the summer of 2018. I last saw my stepfather's acoustic in Paris in late 2009, at my friend from Chambana Jayson's flat. The song remains the same.

Also on October 6, 2020, the world lost Champaign–Urbana rock legend Angie Heaton. In the '90s, Angie shredded the drums in the band Corndolly, as well as recorded CDs with Angie Heaton and her Gentle Tamers. We didn't hang out a lot, but we moved through the '90s Chambana band scene at the same time. So much more than a stalwart mainstay of the scene, Angie wrote killer songs and was a hoot to be around. I fondly recall her performing as Stevie Nicks *and* Ozzy during the years the rock club Mabel's put on The Great Cover-Up. Though of course not trending the way

EVH is today, Angie Heaton's music is also shredding on YouTube for all eternity.

> Our grief is
> as multilayered
> as our lives.
> The heart of
> grief is where
> we might find
> the deepest in-
> sight into what
> really matters.

Then yesterday, October 7, I found myself crying in front of the TV yet again, this time while witnessing two longstanding world records fall on a track in Valencia, Spain. The women's 5K world record is now 14:06.65, as Letesenbet Gidey smashed Tirunesh Dibaba's 2008 time by five seconds. During the bell lap, I started clapping and cheering as if I were there, and by her final stretch I was bawling. It was a singular and beautiful performance, followed by Joshua Cheptegei smashing the 10K world record by over six seconds. The twenty-three-year-old Ugandan ran an unfathomable 26:11 flat to better the great Kenenisa Bekele's 2005 time. As with Gidey, I cheered myself hoarse during the bell lap and sobbed my way through the final couple hundred meters.

I'd like to say that I went out for a run afterwards, but I didn't. Maybe today.

Sean Connery famously confessed that he only cries at sporting events, and I find a similar catharsis at work when channeling the lives of other animals, witnessing great feats in athletics, or listening to music. Grief and ecstasy are intimately related; both make you feel outside of yourself, both push you to explore the profound depths of otherness within each one of us. When I run, I am putting all of these elements of consciousness into conversation with each other.

Shredding as catharsis cannot occur in isolation, but only in relation, as running encourages an elemental empathy for others. The Jewish theologian Martin Buber refers to such a phenomenon as an I-You (Ich-Du) relationship, a dynamic and intersubjective moment of awakening that overrides the I-It (Ich-Es) relationship that defines the alienating "itification" of everyday life. One moves beyond the "itifying"—also referred to as reifying—tendencies of consumer capitalism, which sees the entire world solely through the lenses of profit, product, and proliferation, and into a realm where something else is going on.

Only in the realm of the I-You relationship can we save the planet and ourselves with it, and the powers that be have figured out that it is in their best interest if this relationship is curtailed. After Buber, French theorists like Deleuze & Guattari and Paul Virilio, as well as American thinkers like Cornel West and Chris Hedges, have articulated the totalizing and overwhelming parameters of the I-It relationship under global capitalism. To shred is to run towards a dynamic and harmonious being-in-the-world, the I-You relationship.

The Beatles have intimated a way for you and me to come together: "I am he as you are he and you are me and we are all together." It is no coincidence that this revelation comes out of the acid trip and the looney bin, so pervasive are the alienating imperatives of the so-called rational world to deny the I-You relation, the elemental and instinctive truth that you are me and we are all together, that our distinctions ultimately and elementally don't make a damn bit of difference.

In 2013, I cried in front of this same TV watching the stock footage of the Boston Marathon bombings over and over. And I cried watching the footage over and over of Meb Keflezighi crossing the finish line in 2014, the first American to win Boston since Greg Meyer in 1983. That year, over 70 percent of Boston participants were first-timers, myself among them. Six years and a lifetime later, I return to that race over and over.

Grief and joy go hand in hand. Boston runs as one. We are all the walrus.

With S

Today I cut across
a frat house lawn.
I trod over some
fresh-cut grass but

the nearby University
President was not
available for comment.
I saw then I'd been

wearing Dragon
colors on Bison turf
just past the Bison
Turf. I was thinking

too much about a
train. I had issues
with mud but it was
all good. I had a map

in my head I could
deviate from. I never
truly thought I might
get shot or arrested or

that the walk might
take some wrong turn
just like no one thinks
they will actually eat

shit and die—except
maybe me every now
and again but not right
now. Right now I can

find some pluck in my
walk. I must've crossed
a dozen parking lots just
to put that S in reverse.

Truth be told, I felt it
drawing me drawing it
nearer with every little
hiccup step. I was wearing

the garb of a serious
runner thinking about
S and why and why and
why. All the while the

answer was elemental.
S and I were walking
over one another. This
happened over and over.

SHRED!

October 12, 2020

Not much running this past week; only three days out of seven. After a couple of days off, I ran 7.5 miles at 6:45 pace, and felt great. Then whatever momentum I might have had from running more than five miles went out the window. Two more days off, but managed to get out yesterday for five miles at 6:55 pace, on another ridiculously windy day in Fargo. Somewhere in there I agreed to run a 5K time trial with a mate who wants to get under 18 flat. At this point, I haven't run with anyone in months, so the idea of shredding a 5K sounds fun—until I consider the wind, and how frustrating it is to try to turn it up on a gusty day.

Races are often remembered for the extreme weather conditions that just happen to fall on the day of a major shred. The Grand Forks Half Marathon a few years ago (windy), the infamous Boston Marathon of 2018 (windy, rainy, scary), Grandma's 2016 (hot), the Half Fast Half in February 2013 (3°F at the start), the Ole Man River Half in Gretna, Louisiana (windy): all served up weather that could readily excuse not sticking to one's goal pace. That said, some people (notably, some American women) actually ran PRs at Boston 2018, where conditions felt akin to shellshock for runners and spectators like me and Mom alike.

I fondly recall that my PRs in both the 10K (July 4, 2013; 33:33) and the half marathon (May 2016; 1:14:25) were run in town on very hot days. I don't recall the wind being much of a factor. In both instances, I had reached a point in the training where the urge to shred overruled the more common-sense approach to the conditions. I didn't know for certain how fast I might be able to go, and because of that I maintained a belief that I could run even faster.

Developing a shredding being isn't solely a physical endeavor, and like most people I have to practice believing in myself. I have to train myself to move in harmony through the world. Throughout my life, I have routinely practiced setting limits on what I can accomplish. Forty years after running my first marathon, I must compel myself to be open to the possibility of cosmic harmony, a kind of shredding that ventures beyond time and into a realm of dynamic intersubjectivity. Ironically, perhaps, a timed race can offer this kind of harmonious relationship between the earthly and unearthly. It is an utterly human, utterly otherworldly kind of sensation.

It occurs to me that I've benefited from remaining intensely curious as to, but stalwartly unaware of, the limits of my body and mind. When I ran my first marathon, three weeks after turning twelve in 1980, I hadn't run longer than seven miles. I really had no business registering for such an ordeal, but truth be told, I think more about the magic that resulted from that rash decision than I do about the potential harm I did to my growing body. Both may come up in the mental conversation, but I only listen to the magic.

I don't know how long I stared at the ad for America's Marathon—which is what the Chicago Marathon was originally called—in *Running Times* that year, or how many weeks before the race I sent in my registration. Remember having to mail in registration, anyone? I just remember a half-page ad with the tagline TO RUN IS TO WIN. If you're new to the game, as I most certainly was, this takes a while to unpack.

I didn't know anything about pacing or The Wall, certainly nothing about proper fueling. It was 1980, after all. I was barely twelve years old and weighed well under 100 pounds. Did I even have a decent pair of running shoes?

I remember it taking me several minutes to get to the starting line, and I have some blurry recollection of the city and the course along the way. Those were the days when Mom could cheer me on from several vantage points before I reached the finish line, where there were no barriers between spectator and participant.

I have a memory of the late stages of the race, when a young Black volunteer ran after me with a cup of water. Our age and the event united us in a way that the color of our skin and (sub)urban planning would segregate us over the next forty years. As it happened, my main Chicagoland age-group rival would be a POC shredder from Dolton named Joe Lindsay; and the prepubescent/adolescent marathon scene at the time was dominated by St. Louis native Wesley Paul, who had Asian ancestry.

As such, my Midwest neck of the woods was unpredictably multicultural, quite different from the broad brushstrokes that often characterize depictions of the flyover zone. I don't romanticize 1980 as a moment of multiracial American harmony, of course, but I am interested in rediscovering a worldview that frustrates the assumed boundaries of the legacies of race and class. How odd that we unconsciously use the same words to infer competition and culture!

I ended up running America's Marathon 1980 in a tick under 3:29. I crossed the finish line into the arms of my mother, who was all of thirty-six at the time. Thirty-eight years later, two years ago this past weekend, at the age of fifty and on a mere six weeks of training, I completed the Chicago Marathon in 2:55:38, which averages to 6:42 per mile. It was by far the easiest marathon I'd ever run, and I walked away from the finish line drinking a tallboy of Goose Island 26.2 beer. There was no need for a med tent, as in Rome (and Grandma's, and Boston, and New York, and so on), and I caught up with Mom and Lonna in the family meeting area soon after. The winner was Sir Mo Farah, who crossed the finish line around my age in minutes ahead of me.

Mo was born in Somalia and didn't come to the UK until he was nine years old. That he would become a national treasure and be knighted like Paul McCartney and Alec Guinness tells us something about the elusive, shapeshifting nature of race and racing. Our own American legend, the Olympian and aforementioned Boston 2014 champion, Meb Keflezighi, lived in Eritrea until he was eleven years old. His 2:08:37 time that year at Boston was a personal record, achieved just shy of his 39th birthday. As for myself at Boston in 2014, I ran significantly faster than at Chicago four years later, crossing the finish line some thirty-six minutes behind Meb (in 2:44:49).

Come to think of it, my age in minutes behind the leaders of a marathon seems a decent and random enough time to strive for. More importantly, I'm interested in unlearning what adulthood has suggested I can't do, as well as seeing how far I'm willing to run to regain the belief that I can make a difference in the race of life, that behind the curtain of chaos and crisis lies an elemental harmony moving at the pace of empathy.

October 13, 2020

Three weeks until the most farcical election of recent memory—and I voted in 2000, mind you. But I'm not here to laud any apocryphal moral high ground taken by the Democrats, or pander to the supposed greatness of a country touted by Republicans, when the American two-party duopoly seems simply unwilling and unable to provide for the basic necessities of We the People. We have two major political parties with roughly the same ideology and beholden to the same corporate and military interests: both parties support fracking, both parties are heavily invested in endless war as well as shipping jobs overseas, both have separated families at the border and put them in cages, neither is interested in the slightest in giving people a living wage or health care like the rest of the industrialized world. I have watched the greatest minds of my generation—many of them dear friends—on Facebook make believe that all this started four years ago. Isn't it pretty to think so?

From Ginsberg and Hemingway, I return to Whitman's belief that we contain multitudes. You wouldn't know it from mass media today, which broadcasts the dreams and desires of the one percent (RIP David Graeber, author of *Bullshit Jobs*) until you believe they are your own. I hope I've spent my adult life in the classroom teaching something antithetical to the insatiable impulses of late-stage capitalism, something as elemental and simple as the books you read and the words you learn can set you free. Runners instinctively seek out mantras, not jingles.

The two elemental practices of reading and running can actually be hindered by the screen, that McLuhan-esque medium that insidiously inserts itself to broadcast its message of consume, consume, consume. In addition, we have diluted the message such that consuming it is the easiest thing imaginable. You don't have to waste time considering the myriad resonances and nuances of your native tongue. Eventually, if you scroll, text, or click long enough, you don't need to consider much of anything, certainly not the long and boring history of the word "consider," or its linguistic counterparts "considered," "considerate," and "consideration." As "translation" derives from the expression "to carry across," I wonder if "consider" involves something coincidental, and by that, I mean "co-incidental," maybe a kind of inside that we might both inhabit together. To gather together. To consider something could actually be a way of saying "I think, therefore I am with you," with considering being cast as the most intellectual and intimate of ways to share the same headspace of another being.

Of course, I just tried to google the etymology of "consider," but for some reason couldn't get online to perform the necessary research to reduce or explain away my dynamic flight of fancy. Make no mistake: we have been autocorrected.

Perhaps the most oft-quoted line of poet Louise Glück, who recently won the Nobel Prize for Literature, is: "We look at the world once, in childhood. / The rest is memory." And the much-maligned humanist Karl Marx wrote that history happens first as tragedy, then as farce. I carry these snippets of discourse—ephemeral and eruptive short forms of deep and considered insight—with me across the dying planet.

I thought I might write today about my issues with all versions of the afterlife, an existential conundrum that plagues me most nights, while politics and the dying planet typically occupy my headspace during the day. Then perhaps I'd segue into an assessment of dementia seven years on from Lonna's mom's diagnosis. Because I restarted running avidly in 2012, around the time when we began having concerns about Beth's cognitive state, I often connect the two co-incidentally. Running—as well as our crazy cat Woodman, who has currently forced the computer off my lap and onto the decidedly less-comfortable-to-type-on armrest—came with the dementia in this sense, a concomitant searching for connection beyond the illusory confines of one's individual body and mind.

When I speak of singularity, I don't mean individuality. Individuality is isolated, monochromatic, lonely. Singularity is dynamic, intersubjective, collective. Bringing myself into dynamic harmony with Beth, as well as the world, is akin to speaking an ancient vernacular, tapping into some thrumming primal tongue in which the elemental and oceanic depths of our being beyond language creates an intersubjective space we can inhabit together. The language of we, the breath of life.

Without being aware of its happening, we learn to be satisfied with a debased and diluted mother tongue. Words become obstacles to rather than conduits for revelation. Big words or arcane expressions come to be seen as suspicious, pretentious, yea, even unnecessarily recondite or obfuscatory. This is all going to be on the test.

Falling in love with a word or expression reminds us of how we come into the world of language: with a childlike reverence and astonishment for what words have to offer. We don't say to ourselves, "Gee, I wish we didn't have so many ways to describe what we see or how we feel." Until we do.

Similarly, we don't show up to life with the desire to sit on the sofa while scrolling and clicking the years away. At some point in the journey, we learn to hate our bodies, to see them as obstacles hindering us from full participation in the elemental and instinctive urge to be in motion. Physical activity slowly and inexorably becomes something other people do.

If life was a tradeoff—say, give up physical activity for a full life of the mind, or give up intellectual pursuits for an invigorating and stimulating physical life—our choice to take a particular fork in the road might make sense. But

> because the powers
> that be have
> determined
> that we should
> give up on both
> body and mind,
> we do.

One of my main issues with the afterlife and dementia is that they both seem to require that you give up (on) your body and mind, i.e., that outrageously and singularly beautiful confluence of possibilities that makes all of this possible. Every day that I open up this computer or lace up my running shoes, I begin answering the question: what am I going to do about life's course (coarse) requirements?

October 19, 2020

As I write on this Monday morning, the sun has crept out and proven its point once again: sunlight is crucial for my sense of well-being. A couple hours earlier, I turned on the seasonal affective disorder lamp for the first time. I honestly don't know if it works or not, but I figure twenty to thirty minutes of box light on my left side in the mornings doesn't hurt my chances of avoiding a gray, wintry funk for the rest of the day, or week, or year . . . or pandemic, which could easily last through the winter. Already spring conferences and marathons are being canceled or postponed until fall, just like this year. Fargo winters entail elements of quarantine to begin with, and October can bristle with the pending inevitable sub-zero days of ice and snow ahead. The unanticipated nature of coronavirus in March was especially heartbreaking around here, as we'd just yet again survived a good five months of effective quarantine, albeit regularly broken by pints at the Junkyard and five-mile shreds on a treadmill at the YMCA.

The lizard part of my monkey brain could start worrying about how I'm going to make it through *this* winter without access to a community treadmill. I still don't feel it's safe or prudent to work out at the Y, though some of my friends have and do, and I can't imagine buying one of these behemoths and putting it in the dreary unfinished basement, amidst the washer, dryer, and unused band equipment. I don't think there's an SAD lamp big enough to get me through a five-mile workout in those conditions. Maybe with some throw rugs and mood lighting . . . but still, I'll pass.

After a few gray days of no running, I managed to make it outside yesterday for four miles at 7:02 pace. I didn't want to go out. I had to go out, or else risk that feeling of failure for giving up on running yet again, just when I'm starting to see results in body and mindset. And though we'd had a blanket of snow to go with several gray days in a row, and though my phone said it was freezing but felt like 21°F, due no doubt to the ubiquitous and ridiculous wind, the story of that four miles was classic in structure: negativity and resistance of the "why bother?" variety for the first mile or so, and then intentionality and purpose for the rest.

At some point, I always realize it's all worth it, that four lousy miles on a Sunday isn't merely all I could cough up all weekend long. It was, elementally, the best thing I could've done at that point in time. I wasn't worried about the coming winter, nor was I concerned with my lack of training this past week. There was me and the urge to shred.

Still, I woke up today feeling slightly ill, that kind of low-grade, under-the-weather logy feeling, no doubt due to the dryness inside, as well as getting used to the seasonal changes in general. Because I've proven—yet again!—how easy it is for me to fall off the shred-wagon, it's probably time for me to commit to running at least two miles a day every day. I almost always end up running longer; the two-mile commitment serves as a baseline to get me out there.

I commit to two miles because, when I first started my streak in August 2018, Sally from Beyond Running had committed to two miles, rather than the official streaking minimum distance of one mile. This makes sense for me, as the first mile or so almost always involves wrestling with those negative demons alluded to above. By two miles, I can call it a day, but I often end up adding on at least a mile or two. Given that fifteen to twenty minutes of running might be my only time outside on any given day for the foreseeable future, it makes sense to commit to suiting up and slogging through a workout every day of the week. As with yesterday's run, the results of this commitment are almost immediate.

I keep relearning how easy it is to become sedentary, to become inexplicably and stubbornly insistent that one is not into running or indeed any other exercise. This capitulation to indolence seems to come from both personal negative reinforcement and observing the contemporary American landscape, which all too often privileges binge-watching on the couch, all too often paired with scrolling and glossing our way through the manifold pressures to consume, consume, consume. Of course, I'm offering this anti-capitalist diatribe from the comfort of an archetypal slacker sofa mere feet away from a flat-screen TV (albeit both are hand-me-downs). I'll be here all pandemic!

Only a couple weeks ago, I was checking tennis scores on my phone while watching two different sporting events on the TV and computer. I had turned into my own sports bar. Now when I look up, I see a Chillhop image of a street corner café on a rainy-snowy evening. The café is always open, and even has a jukebox; and though a pickup truck waits around the corner with its taillights flashing, no one ever comes or goes. Living in Fargo during the winter can feel like this.

Weather is as much a projection or self-fulfilling prophecy of our moods as it is something that determines what our moods are.

I know too many people who look forward to winter *and* running, snowshoeing, and skiing through it to feel my fear and loathing of the cold to ultimately have much merit. Of course, it's not as simple as just grooving on shitty weather; but perhaps it's as simple as dressing up appropriately for a playdate with your best frenemy.

Bad weather days can and should also serve as badges of honor. To have survived the nightmare that was Boston 2018—I was already shivering hypothermia-style hours before the start—has turned into a proud accomplishment. I wanted to drop out at every mile marker, but it only made sense to keep moving and make it to the next one. As time and weather slogged on, so did I. I didn't want to risk spending time in a medical tent mid-course just so I could eventually get bussed to the finish line. I ended up running 3:19—not what I'd come to do, but ultimately faster than the year before or after. And at some point, time and weather become mutually irrelevant. The elemental experience takes over, and survival on course becomes a curious lesson about the costs of ecstasy.

And for what it's worth, I beat American Olympian Galen Rupp on that day, as he ended up dropping out. You win some, you lose some, I guess!

The sun is starting to retreat from its morning cameo. I always seem to run at the grayest, windiest, most uninspiring time of the day, and good days mean getting to laugh at the sun's appearance the moment I return from the shred. This happened during last month's 5K time trial, which must have been the dreariest run ever put on by the NOLA Track Club, however unintentionally.

Most days, I can't muster up the requisite belief to benefit from a pithy adage along the lines of "run with the sun in your heart." But I do remember a run last winter with the Beyond Running crew that I keep in my mental arsenal when I feel like I'm losing the endless war against winter. It was a Saturday morning run, the first in many weeks for me. The world had been gray and cold forever, and it took all I had to get downtown on time. I commented to stalwart shredder Marty Lehman about the endless gray days, and he quietly concurred. Never negative, never outspoken, and always running toward the silver lining—that's Marty in a nutshell.

We ended up running the first few miles together, say around a 9:30 to 10:00 minute pace, and around three miles in, the sun came out for a couple minutes. We both felt that distant and elusive stranger on our faces at the same time, were both there to acknowledge its presence, and to be utterly thankful for the moment.

Marty Lehman
and I shared
a fleeting moment
of harmony
running together
in the sun,
and it was
so wonderful.

October 20, 2020

Gray, gray, and more gray. Even the pants I put on yesterday were gray. I ran 5.5 miles in a pair of gray and black Brooks with a black base layer and black tights to boot, blending into the brooding gray landscape, the omnipresent, colorless wind whipping around me. Almost two years ago, in January 2018, I bought my first ever brand-new car, a bright orange Subaru Crosstrek. My guy at the dealership, Mathieu Ross, wondered if I'd be interested in a less expensive model, perhaps a white or gray one. At this point, we were only corresponding by email, but I bristled visibly. It had to be the orange car, all the way down to the orange stitching in the interior. Now you see them everywhere.

Normally I've come into used cars, starting with Mom's 1984 baby-blue Chevette, which we christened the Fishmobile in high school. In graduate school, I flipped Mom's red Saturn—remember those?—during a particularly brutal Illinois winter when I was hoping to drive to Arizona and only made it to effing Effingham before finding myself upended on the side of the road. My run for that day consisted of hightailing it on a frontage road to a nearby gas station, adrenaline pumping in flight mode.

Eventually someone gifted me a red Chevy Cavalier, which my friend Dan McGee helped me fix up and which worked for a while until it didn't. Though impressed with Dan's ingenuity—also a Med Scholar, which meant he was getting his medical degree as well as a doctorate in anthropology at the time—I knew from the moment I got my fingers caught in a front strut that I wouldn't become a mechanic later in life.

Dan, who preferred to work on foreign makes, sold me his beige Honda Accord for seven hundred dollars, which I managed to drive to Arizona, only to have to pay more than four hundred dollars to get it to pass Arizona's ridiculously stiff emissions testing. If Arizona was concerned with climate change, I'd be okay with it, but the state is notoriously environmentally unsound, to say the least. The emissions testing ends up penalizing the working class rather than reducing emissions, which the great state of Arizona has no real intention of doing. But I digress.

I bought a used dark-blue Mitsubishi Expo from some acquaintances in Minneapolis, and made it back to Fargo before it needed some electrical work. And the goddamn automated seatbelt on the driver's side eventually stopped working, and because 1999 was one of two years Mitsubishi implemented this dubious technology, fixing the seatbelt would cost over a thousand dollars. But I digress. Eventually I scrapped it and ended up with Lonna's mom's Mazda Protégé once she stopped driving for good in 2013. It was kind of a blue-gray color as I recall, a kind of neither-here-nor-there hue, as unassuming as Bethy herself, come to think of it.

The color of a car has never had much to do with destiny, this I understand, but I wanted to meet the threshold of fifty driving a blaze of color through the seemingly endless gray days of a Fargo winter. God knows how I would handle Portland, Oregon.

It is perhaps both ironic and predictable that, five months after buying the orange Subaru, I would inherit my father's gray Toyota RAV4 from Wilma after he passed. I first drove that car to his funeral.

No, I don't absolutely love my car. I remain steadfastly ambivalent about motor vehicles, though when running I will channel the wonders of machine technology on occasion. I envision the body as an engine with a burning furnace and will utter "active electronics" to encourage my feet and legs to work together, in tandem with my hips and upper half. I'm trying to be intentional about cadence and footstrike, to have the hybrid body be mutually present to itself.

I assume that, for some runners, this intentionality is second nature; the idea of *not* running does not enter the equation, and perhaps body and mind synch up as a matter of course—pun unintended, but I'll run with it. Even if everything, from body type to past performances, to social demographic, points to me being able to run mindfully and ecstatically, my work ethic and belief system often conspire to power down the engine and keep the electronics inactive. Even now, I seem to be ritually restarting from square one, committing to running, then taking a few days off to wallow in the sunless sunroom.

Yesterday I ran 1.5 miles longer than Sunday at 6:41 pace, some twenty seconds per mile faster. It was by far the easier workout. On Sunday, I felt psychologically tentative, again relearning the strenuous joys of physical exercise. The instinctive truth behind George Sheehan's famous dictum of "listen to the body" doesn't preclude the fact that the body is always listening to the mind as well. I'm looking forward to today's workout, even as the gray day and fresh blanket of snow insinuate that it's going to be another long and arduous winter. More snow—up to six inches—is expected by Thursday, but today I'll log a few humble miles before driving my orange car a half mile to restock the fridge with Oktoberfest beer—because all in all, it's still effing October, people!

If I run longer than I drive on any given day, that should be chalked up as a success. Especially in Fargo, but pretty much anywhere in America, runners are pitted against drivers (though, of course, many of us are both at different times). Sure, I've been heckled in Fargo—"moron," "fag," "you're going to kill yourself"—which means at least I'm being seen by the motorized observers of my shred.

I remember my friend Fej's astonishment that I'd run seventeen miles one day; the thought of *driving* seventeen miles was so distasteful to him. But of course, it doesn't translate. In this sense, seventeen miles in a car versus seventeen on foot is *literally* not the same distance.

More importantly, when we drive, we are typically driving alone, the entire endeavor seemingly set up to encourage a peculiarly trenchant and unconscious form of not seeing. Add to that the fact that so many people of all ages can't put down their phones while they drive, and we're only beginning to scratch the surface of how deep and insidious our commitment to unseeing truly is.

On that note, today's acrostic for the Shred is thus: Seeing, Hearing, Relearning, Envisioning, and Doing. It is akin to what the mystics might refer to as tuning in, and it is what happens when we get out of the car and put down the phone and relearn to take in the raw and unfiltered world around us. In this world, there is a scampering rabbit whose side I'm on and a beautiful crow with a broken wing (cue Bob Dylan). Just around the corner, there may be a rafter of turkeys on a residential lawn, or a doe with her fawn in tow. One orange car may not do much set against a gray and desolate environment, but sharing some mad weather while shredding with you might just.

October 21, 2020

Ah, the sun, the sun, the sun: there is no substitute. Looking out the window this morning, I could tell the snow wasn't going to melt, that conditions were going to remain icy, slushy, windy, and generally dreary, but the sun was going to make an appearance. It's in my backyard right now, so I can say "I'm sitting in the sunroom" without the requisite trace of wry irony.

Still, I played a little guitar while sitting next to the SAD lamp, awaiting the real McCoy. As they say in England, it's early doors right now, and yet it could as well be December 21st out there. I think about yesterday's run, trying to be simultaneously cautious and free-flowing, to not tense up on the slushy, icy parts of the course, which turned out to be the entire six miles. I couldn't see very well with the snowy wind getting in my eyes, and I felt ungainly and awkward. And yet I decided to tack on a couple of miles before turning home and regaining my rightful place on the ironically named sunroom sofa.

As with downhills, so with ice. It's important to not put on the brakes when heading downhill, although an icy downhill might mean you have to slow to a tentative walk. Personally, I'm not a fan of slip-on cleats like Yaktrax and the like, but in certain conditions they can certainly help you to trust your footing. Since my first Boston in 2014, I've kept the advice of BAA coach Terrance Mahon in mind, speaking specifically about how to run the course's downhills: make like you're running on eggshells. In practice, this means striking less on the "brake pads" of the heels and more on the balls of the feet, which is one argument for running barefoot as well, as without shoes we are more apt to land mid- to forefoot.

Since coming back into the running fold, I've read a couple great books by dudes who swear by barefoot running, both of them Brits, as it happens. After one of them, *Running with the Kenyans* by Adharanand Finn, I even felt the glee of shucking off the shoes and doing some strides in the park outside Wycliffe Hall in Oxford. I also grew up relishing the story of Abebe Bikila winning the Olympic marathon in Rome in 1960 shoeless. Rome 2013 turned out to be my first marathon in my forties. But in Fargo, for perhaps obvious reasons, it's been more tempting to try out different shoes than attempting to log any serious mileage shoeless.

Pro tip for the seasonal affective disordered lover of sun when that fickle god goes away: put on some Sun Ra, and restart the cosmic sonic dialogue. If your mix then switches to Eno's *Apollo: Atmospheres & Soundtracks* perchance, then by all means go lunar as well.

In 2020, it feels like the current craze of racing shoes with rakish stack heights and tricked-out carbon plates derives from the idea that we can go faster if we simulate downhill running with a built-in starter's block that unflaggingly pushes the runner forward. Without getting into the controversy of whether this new shoe technology gives an unfair advantage to those who wear them—footwear as performance-enhancing clothing, sometimes compared to the crazy swimming suits from a couple Olympics back—I would note that, primarily because of the stack height, such shoes do not perform well on the track or in adverse conditions. Simply, stack shoes plus twists and turns equals rolling an ankle or two.

Just this past weekend, in fact, we witnessed a number of falls during the World Half Marathon Championships in Poland . . . and yet Peres Jepchirchir still managed to set a world record of 1:05:16 for a women-only 13.1 miles. It is indeed an exciting time for global running, and I'm tempted to assert that it has nothing to do with the technology. When you come up with the bright idea of moving forward, of putting one foot in front of the other for any length of time, something beyond or besides technology is taking place. You become part of the shred.

The shred isn't always pretty, mind you, and it often doesn't feel like something astonishing or even significant is happening. What can a walk around the block do? What can a couple lousy miles a day accomplish, really? Some days I slog through the couple lousy miles and I can't come up with an answer. But by then the questions have changed, and I don't have to pay the cynical and despairing parts of my mind any mind.

And now the sun has come back again. After yesterday's permanent eggshell shred, I can feel new stiffness in my mid and lower back, as well as in the quads and hamstrings, where all the downhills I've ever done live. And though I tried to go as slow and easy as possible, I still ended up running at a 7:29 pace. Today I'll aim for slower and easier, half the distance as yesterday, four miles max.

I'm no chiropractor, but I know these are conditions made for misalignment and subluxation. But the alternative of no motion is way worse. So, despite feeling like I slept funny, enough to compound the overall soreness of the day before, I put my aching back and sore Achilles tendons and niggling left elbow and funky-in-a-bad-way right wrist through the paces of my modest quarantine-era strength workout. A plank or two actually helps release tension from these trouble areas, and to remind body and mind that we're in this together. And I hang out with the sun in its guest room.

Ultimately, running is not about becoming faster, which may seem contradictory to the uninitiated, just as the aim of haiku poetry is not about concision or explanation, but illumination and expansion. It has nothing to do with summary, but concerns tuning into an aha moment—one beyond rational understanding, beyond mastery—that compels us forward, toward a harmonious enlightenment that comes from 93 million miles away. So here goes nothing:

> We move in a world
> with no fast or slow only
> go and go and go

October 23, 2020

Back in the sunroom, sun in the backyard, and a plumber snaking a drain in the basement. It must be somewhere between five and ten years since I had someone take care of the neighbor's tree roots, which spread underground—can I say shred underground?—at their natural, epic pace in contravention of property lines—which, all things considered, are the proverbial new kids on the block in terms of how we see the world, as a land manifestly destined to be divided up and parceled out, private property an inalienable right, as the indicator and dictator of progress.

I always seem to mentally call out the neighbor for the natural urges of the tree, which isn't truly owned by anyone, it is just Tree, just as I call out the apple tree in the *other* neighbor's backyard every other summer for breaching the fence line. One summer, around a dozen years ago, we had a groundhog living beneath the porch who would eat apple after apple from that very tree that a previous owner—that word again—had planted for his spouse twenty or so years before I moved to the neighborhood in the summer of 2003.

Like finding a language beyond language to commune with Beth, my goal is to move in harmony with the groundhog. I observe the critters who carve out an existence amidst the incursions of human beings, with their plumbing and their cars and their construction, which proceeds apace with the profit motive that compels so much of human endeavor. At the same time, however, there is Tree pace, Groundhog speed, and Apple time.

Yesterday I ventured into the gray and dismal world for a few miles, and was surprised to discover I felt more than good a mile in. By mile two, I must have been smiling into the wind while listening to my snow-crunching footfalls by the high school. With the wind at my back, I picked up the pace naturally and figured I might as well run a little longer. I wanted to see what running across the giant berm by the baseball field would be like with a fresh coat of powdery snow. It is not lost on any runner in this area that the white majesty of Snow pace soon turns into the gray, traffic-inflected mundanity of Slush pace. It's a blessing to get out there before the cars do.

By mile three, I was having one of those shreds you want to tell a fellow runner or loved one about. We've all had them, those miles when we're so in the zone that all the worries of the day become inconsequential. These runs may come few and far between, and they always show up unannounced, but they're reminders—I should say epiphanies—of how we reacted to the wild and unpredictable world of childhood. Of *course,* I want to stay outside and play in the snow some more. It just feels so . . . life-giving, so natural, so intrinsic to being human. If you run with a group, you probably thank each other for the run at its end. When sharing the road, we share something singular and momentous, and we give our best selves to one another, dynamically embodied beings in empathetic motion.

I often think of the deep truth regarding seeing that Trinidadian-born Nobel Laureate V. S. Naipaul offers in his description of colonized "mimic men": we become what we see of ourselves in the eyes of others. I've always read this sentence through the lens of (British) colonialism, as a colonial gaze that imposes cultural imperatives that the colonized "others" of empire must mimic in order to assimilate, akin to psychiatrist and cultural critic Frantz Fanon's assertion in his seminal work *Black Skin, White Masks*: "*il n'y a qu'un destin pour l'homme noir, et il est blanc*" (there is only one destiny for the Black person, and it is a white one). But today I wonder about the possibility of reading our "becoming what we see in the eyes of others" as more akin to Buber's I-You relationship, more like what happens during a long run with others, when the trappings of so-called normal human commerce start to fall away, and a different kind of communing comes into play. I shred unto you as you shred unto me.

In addition to this reverie, I was also bemusedly wondering why we're typically assigned Jack London's "To Build a Fire" sometime during the tender grade-school years. Is it taught as a cautionary tale about not going into the woods alone? Or are we supposed to connect winter and mortality as something that awaits us all, something that we can't outrun? One lesson I gleaned from the short story back in the day: if your spit freezes before it hits the ground, you're fucked. Maybe high schoolers are reading Jon Krakauer's *Into the Wild* these days, a similar saga which speculates strikingly about the final hours of a young man who wanted to live off the grid, but because of a few twists of meteorological fate, knows that his time has come.

Right before the berm, I ended up twisting my ankle. I knew it was more serious than minor, but it also felt like I could keep going on it and it might "work itself out." Clearly, I'd been watching too much soccer; I might have to step off the pitch for a half-minute or so, but there was no way I intended to be subbed out and sent to the showers early. Not when everything had been going so well, and it was so obviously my day to be in the zone.

First thought: of *course*, I twist my ankle now, right when I thought I had a shred going to tell Mom about. Second thought: I should just walk it home, a mile away. Third thought: I might as well take the berm while I'm here, as long as I'm able, as long as it doesn't hurt *too* much. And it didn't. Not really.

Then I slipped and fell on the berm, the makeshift path atop it obscured by the snowfall. No big deal, keep going. I slipped again towards the end of the jaunt, maybe a quarter-mile stretch, but managed to stay upright. And by the end of the 5.5 miles at 7:04 pace, I wondered if all those perfunctory ankle lifts I'd been doing at the end of workouts actually strengthened my ankles enough to negotiate this kind of situation, which is to be expected . . . well, for the next six months, actually. Sigh.

But, as was to be expected, the ankle tightened up several hours later. One minute you're on the couch with the flush of the great outdoors on your rosy cheeks, the next you're hobbling to the freezer for the ice pack. The kicker is that I didn't slip on hidden ice or land weirdly on uneven pavement or do anything that I'd successfully avoided doing all week. And today, after icing the ankle again in the morning and testing it throughout the day, I have to say it's best to take a day off, maybe even two. So much for streaking.

I mean, I could've jogged a couple miles this afternoon without making matters much worse—*probably*—but then the sewage hit the fan, and two o'clock hit with me eating nothing, cleaning up muck in the basement, and cursing myself out for not being able to reattach the goddamn dryer vent or whatever it's called. One minute I feel like I can shred destiny, the next I feel woefully inadequate to address the very basic tasks at hand.

The other kicker is that today turned out to be the sunniest day all week, and I really only left the house to run out a check to the guy for services rendered. As it happened, I didn't have to wait all afternoon for Godot to fix the problem, as is so often the case. You know the drill: we will show up between ten a.m. and four-thirty p.m. (if at all!).

And so I went upstairs for a half hour catnap with Gracie, aka Cakey Sweets, the seventeen-year-old sister of Hero (RIP). Often when I head up to the running room to get ready to go out, Gracie will make her priorities clear, and my run will be waylaid, sometimes as long as a couple of hours. But there is something singular and soothing and elemental about synching up with Cat time—and moving at Gracie pace.

October 26, 2020

This morning, I finished folding the laundry I put in yesterday, as well as some of Lonna's that she'd done. I took the garbage to the edge of the driveway in the alley, put away the dishes from last night's pasta feed—not really a *feed* per se, just some leftover linguini with a jar of store-bought pesto and the rest of the store-bought tomatoes over-ripening on the counter, but with fresh garlic and olive oil. For some reason, it feels good to imagine Sunday evening as the night before Marathon Monday, as Boston is known, the time where you do your best to dispel all the demons and dread that start to creep in over the weekend, and before embarking on a singular and epic journey. Instead of Boston, however, it's just another marathon Monday, the beginning of week X in the interminable pandemic training cycle.

Sundays and I have never gotten along, this despite the fact that every day I pay homage to that celestial body called the sun. Sometimes I think I can blame it on Catholic school, but it probably started even before first grade at Our Lady of the Wayside, i.e., during the mid to late '70s when I got my first pair of glasses, as well as had my first crush (which I nurtured for years in silent and unrequited agony, at least until moving to public school in the suburb next door in fifth grade allowed me to move on). Rather than appreciation for the sacred nature of the Lord's Day, I instead ended up cultivating a keen and eerie dread for the profane week about to begin.

During my coming-of-age years, Al Jourgensen, formerly of Ministry, famously sang that every day is Halloween, just as Morrissey, formerly of The Smiths, famously sang that every day is like Sunday. I love The Velvet Underground's "Sunday Morning," which I associate with the undergrad years in Madison (1988–91), as well as Johnny Cash's version of Kris Kristofferson's "Sunday Morning Coming Down," which always brings me back to grad school days in Champaign–Urbana (1992–2000). Both tunes perfectly capture the regular heartache that comes at the end of the weekend. Even though I'm not teaching right now, even though I really have nowhere to go at present, and even though I spent the entire weekend nursing my ankle while watching other people engage in sports in mostly empty stadia, I know classic Sunday dread when I feel it.

But, like the wind and the gray, even Sunday can be seen as a frenemy these days, a day to let myself off the hook and practice being totally okay with not getting anything done save mentally and physically preparing for the following day, i.e., Monday, the day of the moon. The epic dialectic between moon and sun—philosophical kin to the phenomenal dualism of yin and yang, as well as the materialist dichotomy between home and work elaborated by Marx—defines how we collectively imagine the temporal parameters of human interaction and meaning.

These abstract words allow me to articulate a hallowed substrate of consciousness feeding our waking experience. Runner's mind—the mind of shred—means listening to the body, to be sure, but the body as a cosmic tuning fork vibrating on the cusp of an epic time signature, hearing the heart of the heart of shred.

Only upon rewinding the mix tape of memory do I realize how this dualistic struggle is written into the linguistic fabric of how we ritually and routinely—for ritual and routine are intimately connected as well!—experience recursive time, how we make sense of and cope with the brutal nature of linear time hurtling ever faster into the future. In linear time, we are simultaneously compelled to leave the past behind as "ancient history" and imagine the present as a kind of temporal vessel whose sole purpose lies in shuttling us to the "not now" of the weekend, holiday, retirement, or end of the pandemic. More immediate and more important than imagining a future with no problems—keeping in mind that "utopia" means both "the good place" and "no place"—we reset the week on the bended pendulum of sun and moon.

There has been plenty of sun on this particular moon day, so I didn't have to nuke myself (another revealing slang verb, courtesy of the Atomic Age) with boxed light as I did yesterday. I made coffee, and then made pizza dough. I usually wait to make dough until the afternoon, but this morning I just felt like feeling the mundane pleasure of making something out of nothing. Of course, I know it takes flour, olive oil, yeast, and water to make dough, but something ineffable and immediate comes out of mixing these few elements, and transforming them into dough, literally kneading the dough into existence. I can tell when I've got the right proportions of everything, when the yeast has been properly heated, and when the inherent sponginess of dough is starting to announce itself.

That sponginess is the heart and soul of dough, the indomitable pizza spirit arriving *ex nihilo, deus ex machina*. It is perhaps why during certain holidays Jews eat unleavened bread, to honor the ancestors who sacrificed their lives so we could partake of the sacred yeast of deity. I'm riffing on what I gleaned from the '80s and my two Jewish stepfamilies, neither of whom were exactly orthodox practitioners of the faith, but each certainly influenced my inchoate heterodox belief system on where soul or spirit might be found.

As runners, we become particularly attuned to recursive and ritual passages of time. We imagine incremental progress through twelve-, fourteen-, or sixteen-week training cycles (they are called "cycles," after all) that ideally keep us from getting ahead of ourselves, and which encourage us to believe in the elusive improvements of the day-to-day wax and wane of distance running. In this ritual/routine, we find our reason for being. And to paraphrase what Beyond Running employee and Olympic Marathon Trials qualifier Maddie Van Beek once told me, "Fitness comes from strange places at strange times."

To fitness, I would add revelation, because we are training for that as well. And what is the pace of revelation? If we go out too fast, the marathon will more often than not make us pay for it, and sooner rather than later. If we try to get fit extra fast, or to recover too quickly from a grueling race, we may end up experiencing a training setback greater than the sum of our daily bread and butter. I know I'm mixing metaphors here, or perhaps I'm kneading them into a workable weekly dough, something to keep me present and alert to the potential for transformation, insight, revelation, harmonic convergence.

Now the only thing missing from today is the run itself. I've spent several hours listening to Afrobeat, Voodoo Funk, and Electronic Mystic music on YouTube, in the hopes of writing myself into a kind of mental fitness that comes from playing with words while basking in the sun. The music takes me back to Senegal in 1996, the only time I've set foot on the African continent, and which taught me so much about music, life, and movement. Similar to Sicilians, I suppose, Senegalese people seem to show up in the strangest places. That's my tongue twister for the day, at least.

On the other side of Africa from Ethiopia and Kenya, the proverbial hotbeds of global running, Senegal has no Kenenisa Bekele or Brigid Kosgei—nor did they make it out of the group stage in the 2018 World Cup, for that matter—but I recall many evenings by the Atlantic watching the runners put in the miles up and down the coast road that leads from downtown Dakar to the airport, myriad recursive runners returning to town week after week. I never joined them, but I wish I had.

Perhaps one day I shall return to the land of hospitality, or *reewu téranga*, as Senegal is known, eat *ceebu jën* with *samay xarit* and dance to *mbalax* music until the sun goes down. I know that every run I do today allows me to return to those early days of language learning—including English—when I didn't know what I was doing, and before I could express what music or words or running did to me. Before I knew that Monday follows Sunday as sure as the day is long.

November 1, 2020

I wanted to want to run a marathon yesterday. I half-wanted to be in half-decent shape to pace the three stalwart dudes from the Beyond crew who decided to brave the hilly Detroit Lakes, Minnesota, course (basically two rolling-hill-laden laps around the lake) yesterday, Halloween morning, at least for one of the laps.

In years past, the Dick Beardsley Half Marathon would fall on the weekend closest to my 9/11 birthday, and I have fond memories of the four times I've run the race, which includes the real Dick Beardsley, in flesh and blood, a midwestern marathon hero if ever there was one. In 2012, the Dick Beardsley Half Marathon was my first attempt at the distance as an adult, and like child, like adult, I didn't know what the heck I was doing and went out too fast, still managing to take tenth place in 1:23 and change, albeit being passed by local and regional shredder Troy Ivesdahl in the final mile. I would eventually learn that Troy is a dude who knows how to pace himself, someone who can always keep it together enough to drop a sub-3:00 full. Seriously metronomic.

Then the following year I took second in 1:16 and change, and "met" my childhood hero Bill Rodgers ever so briefly at the typically poorly attended awards ceremony. I've noticed how, in this day and age, that awards ceremonies, should they be held at all, don't usually have the same communal feel from days past. Maybe it's just my rose-colored childhood glasses fogging up, but it seems that a lot of this vibrant kinetic energy surrounding the race itself is channeled—I would even say diverted—toward the online experience. I'm sure I'm not the only one who's noticed how we pore over the spreadsheets posted on the wall of the clubhouse, if they are printed out, or line up, ideally beer in hand, to print out splits, place, age group stats, and overall time from the computer gurus at the tent. It's a kick, often more meaningful than the commemorative swag.

But the bigger the race, the more likely the awards ceremony turns into something for snail mail. The bigger the race, the less likely you are to be *allowed* to linger, in fact, else you keep kissing that Boston finish line over and over. In Chicago, forty years ago and barely twelve years old, I crossed the marathon finish line running into the arms of my thirty-six-year-old mother. Come to think of it, there was no awards ceremony then, either—but Mom being there was enough. I wouldn't mind if I could google it, to be completely honest.

When I finish a race, I usually want to hang out for as long as possible. I want to hug a volunteer or three, and be on my third beer and/or donut by ten a.m. And more and more, it seems that the party has become more of a perfunctory rarity or a privatized phenomenon.

Because of my birthday, the Dick Beardsley Half has always been a great excuse to get a hotel the night before and hit up the Fireside Restaurant for a birthday dinner pre-shred. Why not make a weekend out of a race? And still, most people in town get up early, drive to Detroit Lakes, run the race, and can get back to Fargo–Moorhead well before noon. It's not about the medal or the t-shirt, after all.

In 2017, just before turning forty-nine, I took 4th Place at Beardsley after Adam Pangrac and Ben Melby (both of the Beyond crew) and Brandon Scheel (running his first ever half and taking third in under 1:15). I had a ridiculous and ridiculously itchy beard, more salt than pepper, and by mile four was easily dropped by my fellow compatriots of shred. I've often quipped since that day that I'd considered guilt-tripping the three dudes I spent the first three miles with to let the old man get to the podium, but the truth is that I murmured to Brandon that I wasn't going to be able to keep up a 5:30 pace for very long. I was right. And still, Mom was there for this one, not having watched me shred a half marathon before. No matter how it goes, I always look better towards the end of a half than a full. And I managed to dial in a 1:16:30, and without vomiting directly onto Brandon Scheel's shoes immediately thereafter—but only just.

When putting in forty to fifty miles a week, I feel quite capable of dialing in a half between 1:25 and 1:30. But then I must confess that, as much as I love the tradition of running Dick Beardsley, I've never really gotten behind the Detroit Lakes course wholeheartedly, most especially if it's a windy day with good ole Midwest mistrals whipping around at 25–30 mph, as was the case yesterday. Then again, the natural weirdness of having a half around a lake with an opening couple of miles in town is certainly part of the singular charm. You know the course isn't especially fast or forgiving, but at least it's funky and cool (in 2019 I even had two motorcycle escorts!) and so DB is perhaps the closest I've come to understanding the irrepressible centripetal force that draws everyone to Lakes Country around here.

Last year I ran a tick under 1:19 and took second, after Adam, who won for the third year in a row while shredding a 1:13 PR on that frustratingly hilly and windy course. So, maybe don't listen to a word I say.

True to diversifying form, this year was supposed to include a 25K to celebrate the 25th anniversary of the event. With the change in ownership a few years ago, they've also tried adding a full marathon, a 10K, a dog run, a beer run, and even a bicycling event during the week, in the hopes of generating new enthusiasm for a traditionally unassuming and classic old-school regional race. I can't say it's worked. I have a theory about how trying to offer a race experience for everyone actually ends up compromising the race experience for everyone. But having a 25K one year? Fine, go for it.

The quixotic singularity of a half around Detroit Lake the weekend after Labor Day occurs right around the time when the weekend warriors concern themselves with taking in the pontoon dock for the season. That is also the spirit that motivates the marathoner in a time of pandemic, the ridiculous urge to inaugurate a new and unsponsored running tradition, to "go Barkleys," as it were, by running the Detroit Lakes Halloween Marathon, which is twice around that eerie lake in that most scary of years known as 2020, a lake as hallowed and ominous as Loch Ness in Scotland, when you come to think about it—which also has a nice marathon to its credit, I've been told. That's the kind of foolish and impetuous endeavor I can get behind. But then part of me must still be recovering from Boston 2018.

I hear the whipping
wind and see
the gray expanse
of gray, and want
nothing more
ambitious than
to lock into
Gracie pace.

A Brief Essay on Food and Water

In Africa, a mommy elephant may eat
her dead baby so that scavengers cannot.

In 1932 and 1933, people in the Ukraine
were so hungry they abducted and ate

other people's children, and I suspect
that they sometimes had to eat their own.

A mommy ant will eat as many of her
newborns as it takes until she has enough

protein in her to give life to the colony.
If there is one thing I've learned on this

brief jaunt through contemporary history,
it is that people will eat just about anything

to survive. They will eat tree branches as
well as dig up the carcasses of dead horses

if it means that they might make it through
another inhospitable winter. Women in

Kenya are waiting hours maybe days by
a well so that they may take home some

water for their families. We all know that
water is even more important than food

in that one can go a month or so without
food if it comes to that, but if you go a week

without water you will surely die. We all
know that the Earth is mostly water and

that we are mostly water, and this surely
means that water is the new oil. To give

but one brief example, a couple living in
southern California owns the rights to Fiji

bottled water, which actually comes from
Fiji in a trademarked rectangular bottle and

can be found in various supermarkets and
convenience stores throughout America.

Some believe that Fiji bottled water is vital
to the Fijian national economy, but it is also

a fact that 53 percent of all Fijians do not have
access to potable water. It must be said that

tourists are strongly discouraged to drink
from the local tap wherever they go, and so

the acquisition of potable (i.e., bottled) water
can become a daily issue for the privileged few

as well. In India, the Coca-Cola Company
has privatized hundreds of miles of the

Ganges River so that they can make and
distribute Dasani worldwide. Now, I won't

drink Fiji or Dasani bottled water because
I happened to be listening to NPR when

they did brief features on these American
corporations. I also won't drink bottled

water that has a Nestlé label affixed to it,
if only for the fact that Nestlé pushed their

Baby Formula onto mommies throughout
the so-called developing world instead of

just promoting breast milk which, if you
happen to be a mommy, is about as local

and as readily available as you can get.
That said, I know that when I buy a bottle

of water abroad I am buying in to the notion
that general well-being has become a kind

of commodity fetish for those who have
the means to pay for it. I remember walking

around Senegal in August of 1996 looking
to score a few bottles of water to tide me

over until I flew to France the following
month. In Italy, I can read about how the

privatization of water is killing Italy, then
order a bottle of *acqua frizzante* with my meal.

I also caught a brief glimpse of a woman in
Naples walking on her way somewhere with

a baby suckling her left breast and I thought
that that was something you don't see every

day in the States. We all know the expression
is "breastfeeding" in English, and that in

turn brings us back to the idea of food.
A child will eat its mommy's milk as if its

all-too-brief life depended on it, just as
I will suckle a two-liter bottle of water in

my hotel room and then have to wonder
where I might find a good place to pee

when I finally decide to walk on my way
somewhere. It is no consolation that we are

all desperate animals hoping for the two
same damn things: to eat, to not be eaten.

November 2, 2020

Another Monday in the Red River Valley, and the sun I keep going on about is outside in full force. The laundry is hanging or in the dryer, garbage and recycling are ready to be picked up, and last night's dishes are put away. Certainly, the whole day could be spent getting out the vote, but because I am appalled by the records of both presidential candidates, I have moral qualms encouraging people to vote for the lesser of two evils. I've done it many times in the past—Michael Dukakis, anyone?—but after following the primaries and researching the issues for a year and a half, I arrive to election week with a recognizable feeling of futility that comes every four years. We always seem to have strayed further from saving the planet and each other.

This particular election cycle has come with more gaslighting and virtue signaling than any other election to date. I find myself disagreeing with dear friends and political heroes alike on the regular, and so start this week with the feeling that whatever I write about, my worldview will be used to dismiss whatever I've written before about the nature of shred. I can feel the kneejerk reactions that define so-called "cancel culture" working inside me already; otherwise put, the "little fascist within" that French philosopher Michel Foucault wrote about is already judging what I have yet to write. The greedy ego that wants to be admired, or at least read, is trying to decide how to write something publishable, something that can't be deconstructed or discounted—or de-platformed, for that matter. A shred of one's own.

Running-wise, October felt like a kind of holding pattern, like the eighth month of a holding pattern that could easily last eight more. Is your pandemic glass half full or half empty? I ran only eighteen days out of the thirty-one, which means I came up a full week short of my shredding goal for the month. Coronavirus cases are through the roof here and nationwide, so a palpable sensation of futility pervades even the most mundane Monday rituals. My modest goal for the rest of today is to get outside for three easy miles, then shower, maybe shave. Having taken the last couple of days off, part of me is already talking myself out of going out. But it's sunny and in the 50s in Fargo in November, so I know staying inside the rooster coop (as in Aravind Adiga's *The White Tiger*) today would be a colossally bad idea.

Today I feel like delving into politics a little, not to propose running as an alternative or escape from them, but instead to suggest that running—at least as articulated by shredding—offers a kind of socioeconomic interaction that is based in the local and the communal. It can see the value in considering third party options, as well as down-ballot candidates or initiatives, is ultimately anti-corporate (i.e., pro-small and independent businesses), pro-open space (i.e., pro-environment), anti-fast-food consumer culture—and, I dare say, running is inherently for universal health care for all. This is more than a political concept, to be sure. Anyone who's been bitten by the urge to shred has felt the *universal* impulse to be in motion in the world with others, such communing speaking directly to the *health* of the individual, community, nation, and planet, as a dynamic and intersubjective worldview driven by the abstract principle of *care*.

As they say, let me be clear: just as running welcomes people of all ages and backgrounds, runners inhabit all shades of the political spectrum. The Beyond Running crew has die-hard Trump supporters, while many of us stumped for Bernie Sanders four years ago, as well as this time around. Especially for the person who sees Fargo-Moorhead from the outside, perhaps through the lens of the famous film or series—or via You Betcha on YouTube—it is interesting to note that my district in Fargo voted overwhelmingly for Sanders, and that he won the North Dakota primary. The state formerly represented by Democrat Byron Dorgan, author of *Take This Job and Ship It*, is also the state addicted to fossil fuels and fracking, currently celebrating the future arrival of an Amazon warehouse. But when it comes down to it, you could say the same exact thing about California, which has recently approved dozens of fracking permits while using prison labor to fight the forest fires raging throughout the state.

Certainly, I'm generalizing to show how North Dakota, California, or any state, for that matter, ultimately frustrates generalization. North Dakotans are just as likely to ignore or vituperate against Standing Rock and the indigenous struggle for justice as protest police violence while advocating for a Green New Deal. We're still waiting to see the first African American representative serving in the state legislature, and yet the Fargo area is incredibly culturally diverse. From Sudanese Lost Boys to Bosnian expats to Liberian refugees, the settlement of this particular patch of stolen land is shot through with strikingly global migration fluxes.

Running reawakens the individual to the fire within us that allows us to move of our own accord. We still drive cars, of course, but when running we run counter to the late-capitalist, failed-state narrative that drives so much of life in the 21st century. The banks and corporations of the world still get paid, yes—they often sponsor races—but occasionally regular traffic is diverted in favor of a joyous event, often for charity, one in which people generate their own energy, fire up their internal furnace, and brave the singular elements of the day. We know intuitively that business as usual is boring, but it is also insidious in its insistence that what you see is what you get. The idea of status quo isn't inert, but an active undercurrent repeatedly reminding us to not look beyond the shadows on the wall of the cave.

I write in the belief that running can make us realize that it is never what it is. Nor do we ever "just do it," for that matter, not really. My write-in ballot for the day must embody all the empathy I can muster. And it must incorporate your name somehow. Look into this mirror and repeat after me: I am the scribe of shred, and I am not alone.

November 3, 2020

It actually hit the 60s yesterday and today, so I prepped for Election-pocalypse 2020 with a couple of five-mile runs. Yesterday's pace was 6:43, today's 6:52. I could feel it in my legs more today, as I did some strength training before heading out, which includes squatting against the back door for three minutes. Ever since experiencing the downhills of Boston for the first time in 2014, I try to make my hamstrings and quadriceps feel the burn on a regular basis, just to jog my muscle memory a bit (*nota bene*: puns shall continue to come fast and furious at regular intervals). My legs certainly remember the downhills more than the iconic Newton uphills, which turn up around 25K after a mostly downhill first half. Everyone preps for the Newton hills, but close-to-sea-level flatlanders like me need to be told about what a mostly downhill course can do to your hams and quads. Let me tell you: it isn't pretty.

Of course, one can be told something about a course, the experience of a marathon, or just about anything in life, and it won't take. This is where muscle memory comes into play in a dynamic and elemental fashion. As I'm getting back into some semblance of shape, despite having no races on the horizon, my muscles take me back to my finest running moments, like Boston 2014, a recollection which in turn reminds my muscles and me that the power of Boston 2014 is forever within me. It may lie dormant, even for decades, but it's there, waiting to be harnessed for shred.

If the transformative experience of Boston 2014 can announce itself through my legs on the run today, which was just the most basic five-mile workout at exactly three-hour marathon pace—just necessary mental and physical maintenance at the end of the day—what else is lying dormant in my body and mind, waiting to be set into motion?

Running in my fifties encourages me to access adolescence and the early days of shred. The yearning that defined years like 1980 come back to me in muscle memory as well. By twelve years old, I so wanted to run a marathon under three hours, the exact pace of my five-mile run forty years later. I even remember one run, around 1981 or 1982, musing about being my age today. I imagined I would go out for daily five-mile runs around 7:00-minute pace—of course, after medaling in the Olympics and winning Boston and maybe setting a world record or two. I'd keep my fitness up, at least; I'd keep running, for sure. Because I ended up not competing in my twenties and thirties—really, from seventeen to forty-three, it has occurred to me that I'm doing more or less what my teenage self predicted would happen down the road, just without all the glory and accolades along the way.

In the interests of full disclosure—and in the idea of muscle memory as palimpsest—I did run a few races during that mostly idle quarter-century, just not with any competitive spirit or serious training beforehand. I returned to the Condell Distance Classic in Libertyville, Illinois, one year (1988?), which probably had a new name by then. I must have already dropped out of college, and was cheered on by high school friends Des (not Linden, but short for Desmond) and H. In homage to the only academic course I'd managed to finish at DePaul University during winter quarter 1987—a philosophy offering on existentialism—I wrote "I Heart Sartre" in black Sharpie on a regular old white t-shirt. I thought I was being so clever, just like when I painted "This is stupid, I object"—a line from the Psychedelic Furs' eponymous debut—on the back of a tan trench coat I wore most of senior year of high school 1985–86.

Forty years ago, I covered the walls of my basement bedroom with myriad sheets of paper, most of which emphatically declared something along the lines of "Carollo breaks three hours for the marathon!" Currently, I am not quite a blank slate lying in wait: I have one word written on the chalkboard wall of the running room upstairs. You can probably guess which one.

There was a Jingle Bell run in the '90s somewhere, and I have a Christie Clinic t-shirt—were there even tech shirts in the 90s?—from a 5K/10K in Champaign–Urbana, Illinois. But I don't really remember it, not in the way I'm riffing on other races here. Perhaps it takes a modicum of intentionality to commit muscles to memory. Maybe something in me didn't want to care about my running self. I'd left high school competition on bitter terms, and so indeed let the urge to shred lie dormant for decades. Even now, I can feel that ambivalence working through my body and mind. Even now, I wonder if I lack the commitment that my thirteen-year-old self expected of me. So now every time I go out for a run, I honor that kid who knew—viscerally, instinctively, elementally—what the America's Marathon 1980 ad in *Running Times* declared: To Run Is To Win.

Because of having relatives in Denver, I ended up running one Bolder Boulder 10K in the '90s—maybe 1997? You can check it on their website. I don't know what that was about. I hadn't run a 10K in forever, and started back in some corral like HH, i.e., in the middle of the second alphabet or around thirty-four corrals from the front. It was fun, and I ended up passing a lot of people, but for some reason there were no light bulbs or flashbacks, at least none that I haven't been successful at repressing. So why not check the results? This well-known 10K is run every Memorial Day, so like Boston it takes place on a Monday. Also like Boston, the Bolder Boulder typically has more than 30,000 participants and has enshrined its hallowed race history online.

According to the internet, I ran Bolder Boulder in 1999, at age thirty—a mere six weeks after defending my doctoral thesis, as it turns out. My time? 38:21. Hey, that's not bad! And at altitude, too, am I right? The next result from this particular database is from February 2013, a punishing half marathon north of St. Paul that was a mere 3°F at the start.

I ended up taking second in that one (the Half Fast Half) and remember coming upon a younger version of myself who was finishing the 5K and in the lead. As I recall, he looked at me beseechingly in the hope that I wasn't running his race. I assured him I was running the half, but quipped that we still had to kick it in. To which the young shredder solemnly replied, "I know."

A holding pattern isn't the same thing as lying dormant. Every day deepens my commitment to see where all of this is leading, to work to keep body and mind awakened and activated, intently tapping into the dynamic palimpsest of muscle memory, with past, present, and future helically entwined like DNA, the sinews of meaning.

Today is not
some culmination
of a campaign,
but the beginning
of a long struggle:
to survive, to save
the planet, and
to finally see
each other as
we truly are.
Raw, wild,
unmediated
and alive.

November 8, 2020

Another Sunday morning waiting in the sun-poor sunroom to watch another soccer match in a mostly empty stadium on the other side of the Atlantic, replete with the requisite pomp and circumstance while punctuated with prerecorded crowd noise: cheering and chanting that allegedly come from past matches at home. You know the athletes can't hear it, that commentators sometimes have the option of headsets with or without crowd noise, with everyone periodically—poignantly and perfunctorily—acknowledging the marked absence of fans in the stands, and that fact's potential effect on the match at hand. Never has watching the beautiful game seemed so eerie, and so ironically vital to feeling part of a larger community, i.e., the obsessively passionate world of team fandom at large.

When I'm not watching live sporting events or highlight reels of the day, you might catch me watching live footage of a town in the Netherlands, or maybe the George Washington Bridge from the Jersey side. For some reason, it's enthralling to access a live broadcast of the lived reality of somewhere else, to verify through the lens of surveillance that the world outside still exists. Whatever keeps me from feeling further removed from the world at large keeps me tuning in.

This year, elite and back-of-the-pack runners alike have suffered from the lack of competition, which is always also an excuse to commune, to tackle the singular peculiarities of a given course on a given day, and to celebrate our common desire to shred. The idea that we run as one, that on any given day we come together to run the same course—to follow in each other's footsteps both literally and metaphorically—cannot happen virtually. I suppose you could run with crowd noise in the headphones to better simulate the experience of crowd appreciation—which is not always a given on an early Saturday or Sunday morning of a humble local race to begin with—but I doubt anyone has done that (prove me wrong?). The random cheers, signage, and ambient noise are endemic to the experience of putting yourself out there on race day. Whether on the sidelines or in the mix, I love to cheer myself hoarse urging other runners on. The pace or time of a runner doesn't matter to me. The fact that you registered for this race and decided to put yourself out there, regardless of where you find yourself on the road to shred, is the most important thing. It is also the most singular and beautiful thing.

In lieu of competition, elites have recourse to racing against the clock, and a number of blisteringly fast times have come about since the pandemic because of these attempts. And with a number of long-standing world records falling comes a new controversy regarding the pacing technology used to go after them—namely the flashing lights around the track that let runners know to the hundredth of a second where they stand in relation to the world record.

Tennis has incrementally integrated its Hawkeye technology into the game, such that the failings of human observers can be contested by the players, who are granted three challenges per set. In turn, soccer has recently implemented VAR technology to make sure all goals are on the up and up, and it's already dramatically affected play on the pitch and final results on the scoreboard. The players don't ultimately have a say, but as before, their actions can compel an official to take another look at any offside call, questionable challenge, or potential hand ball. Celebrations need be tempered or restrained, lest some invisible-to-the-naked-eye infraction ends up pulling the goal back—which actually seems to happen more often than not—and invariably make you keenly aware of how surveillance technology is rewriting the script, for better and for worse.

I don't have a horse in the race of chasing flashing lights around a track. I'm not sure how visible they are, either, how much someone like Joshua Cheptegei's peripheral vision actually registers when running sixty-second laps over and over. And it is still largely believed that human pacers, despite the difficulties involved with pacing someone like Cheptegei, are desirable, lest the race become too tactical or slow from the outset. At this point, we could get into the new craze for carbon-plated shoes with radical stack heights that increase overall energy return, literal springboards for marathon shredding. As mentioned earlier, these shoes are notoriously unstable on turns, most recently evidenced by the recent half marathon world championships in Poland. You wouldn't want to race in them on the track or take them out for some icy, snowy winter miles.

Watching runners like Joshua Cheptegei and Eliud Kipchoge is captivating in and of itself, regardless of the stage and level of competition. There is something otherworldly about the way they run, the way they make setting a world record look inevitable and effortless. And yet, though pacers can be mechanized and shoe energy return optimized, some elemental aspects of racing can't—and, I dare say, won't ever—be orchestrated: namely, the elements themselves, which so dramatically affected Cheptegei's 3,000m race in Kenya against Team Ingebrigtsen racing in Norway this past summer, as well as Kipchoge's 8th place finish at the elites-only London Marathon.

Meanwhile, my neutral (i.e., Chelsea fan) wish for an entertaining draw between Man City and Liverpool has been granted, although the second half started to drag a bit. It was gushing buckets the entire match at the Etihad Stadium, and Lee Dixon couldn't help gushing about how these miserable conditions were wonderful both for viewer and player. True footballing weather. I suppose eventually they may decide to fake conditions, as in the late Nobel Laureate José Saramago's novel *The Cave*, by randomly calibrating wind and rain machines to simulate the once-typical late fall weather patterns of Merseyside, once the icecaps melt and the entire planet desertifies.

Whether I will long for sub-zero midwinter days if I move out of North Dakota remains to be seen. For now, I take comfort in the fact that, despite the downpour across the pond in the Mother Country, the Fargo sun ended up spreading its fingertips of rose into the wine-dark sunroom. The entire planet and I were deep into the second half, with no substitutions left.

SHRED!

November 9, 2020

I woke up before four a.m. this morning, mind racing, having arguments with friends on an internalized Facebook, that insidious proxy that simulates human contact and sociopolitical interaction. Especially now that we enjoy very little face-to-face contact, the Facebook lives inside me the way imaginary classrooms often do: as a place where maybe I should have said something else or taken a different track to get to the real issues of the day, or alternately as a site of validation where others are compelled to like—or at least respond to—the simulacrum of myself on display. Zoom meetings as well are often individualized scroll-a-thons on cellphones while posting random online clips and articles for the group to gloss, the virtual gathering now an occasion to supplant actual conversation with virtual infotainment snippets.

Of course, we were already doing this before the pandemic. It is typical of your local brewpub and mine alike to have patrons who barely look up from their phones to order a pint. Seriously, some dude-bros or party girls can spend *hours* at Junkyard showing each other things on their phones. Not having the cellphone would be as foreign as taking off the baseball cap or going out without makeup—even more so, I'm afraid. And to be clear, this is not a white, heteronormative phenomenon, but a techno-pandemic that affects all demographics. America is a melting pot of consumer culture and titillating surveillance. America is Orwellian irony embodied; as such, perhaps the most patriotic act in these times is to go against the insidious dictates of the Patriot Act.

In the early morning hours, I typically turn a few pages in an effort to quell the inner monologue in the echo chamber of the soul. This morning's light reading was Camus's *L'homme révolté*, the English translation of which is *The Rebel*, which can't do justice to the wordplay Camus employs with nuances of "revolted" and "revolting," as well as the revealing valences involved with turning, such as "volte-face" ("about-face"). I first read it in undergrad, but don't think I really got it. I remember that Camus offers a critique of Sartre and de Beauvoir, here and in his play *Les justes*, regarding the value of revolution "by any means necessary."

So, not exactly light reading, and not exactly a page-turner. Still, I find that even in the middle of the night on the edge of winter I'm not all that interested in escape or divertissement, although I confess to having high hopes for Martin Amis's latest novel, which I ordered from the struggling Left Bank Books in St. Louis, a bookstore I learned about because of a friend on Facebook, no less! I want to recommit to getting better at foreign languages, the dazzling and unfamiliar beauty of which transcends comprehension. In addition to the new Amis, then, and in lieu of being able to actually go to Norway, I ordered a book on learning Norwegian from Left Bank as well.

I find it hard to fathom that it's already been a year since I visited Kristiansand, Norway, for the first time. The weather was largely gray and dismal, that wet sort of bone-chilling cold that sets in in the 30s and lasts all day. The whole week I only ran once, a morning five-mile jaunt on the shoulder between the river and the workaday traffic. People tell me that Agder is beautiful in the summer, and I believe them. It was eerily beautiful last November as well—no gaggles of tourists necessary.

It is well-known that Norwegians will be out in any kind of weather. They won't change plans because of a little rain, sleet, snow, or wind. Toddlers will put on the appropriate gear and queue up for recess, and women in their 70s will pedal their ancient bicycles up the hill just like they always do. The adage that "there is no bad weather, only bad clothing" is as cliché and given as saying "we have two seasons here in Fargo, winter and construction," though often, like today, we have both at the same time.

The days and nights in Norway were packed with meetings, and it would have been uncouth of me to be late to or politely decline any of them. Being slightly early for all events is also the Norwegian way, and it soon became second nature to show up at fifty-nine minutes and change on the hour for the next one. A year later, I hold that eight kilometers inside me, just like that one sweltering five-mile sweat-fest in Illinois during the summer of 2018 after Dad passed.

I also keep Norway front and center in my heart today by wearing the Stormberg hoodie I procured at the outlet mall there. And though the hoodie serves as the quintessential example of good clothing trumping bad weather, back home I quickly become easy prey for bad habits. I let the wind convince me not to go outside; I allow the inclement weather to determine what kind of day I'm going to have. And though I have very few meetings to be on time for these days, I find it all too easy to turn down the daily shred date with destiny.

Often while reading at four in the morning, I think I might log some miles in a few hours, maybe time it so the sun is coming up when I'm a few miles in. But now the urge has passed, and the gray day has taken over. Lonna, to her credit, has just gone into the thick of it for a few miles. But I have a cat on my lap and a book to write, which is currently a rough draft approaching 26.2 thousand words—not bad for a couple of months' sporadic rumination, I guess. Certainly nothing to be disappointed by.

> That first night
> in Kristiansand,
> I learned my first
> Norwegian phrase,
> an artistic graffito
> outside a theater
> by the quiet water:
> *Hvem er du*
> *når du er*
> *ikke redd?*
> Who are you when
> you're not afraid?
> I have asked myself
> that question ever
> since. And now
> I ask it to you.

November 10, 2020

A quick check on the weather outside—16°F, feels like 11—and I head out for the first morning run in a while. After a few minutes into the wind, breathing into my New Orleans Pride Run balaclava until I have to hack up phlegm, I start to feel the cadence of my natural shredding self. The forecast has Fargo turning overcast mid-afternoon sometime, so after a mile I can't help but relish how warm and content I feel running in the sunlight, how my torso is a churning engine, my lungs a burning furnace, my body from head to foot firing on all cylinders. I don't beat myself up for not running the previous four days; I just embrace the singular nature of this unassuming four-mile pre-chiro jaunt on a wintry morning in the Midwest. Like in the song "Once in a Lifetime" by Talking Heads, my pace was same as it ever was, like internalized clockwork, 6:54 per mile.

Like yesterday, I woke up when it was still pitch-dark out, jaw clenched and existential debate in medias res. A few more pages of Camus and a brief visit from Gracie—she doesn't always stay—and I fell back asleep for one more REM cycle. I could have just made coffee and waited for my 10:40 a.m. appointment, but getting outside on the early side—and for the first time since Thursday!—means I have all afternoon to savor the post-run and post-adjustment endorphins currently emanating from me in the sunroom. Can you feel them? And can you dig it?

The runner's high: as proverbially famous as the long-distance runner's loneliness, it is also loneliness's antidote. My high takes the miles of loneliness and converts them into solitude, a solitude that is not solitary at all, but rather singular and multitudinous, teeming and pulsing in unison, moving in harmony with and between the worldly and otherworldly. Indolence is trumped by purpose and curiosity, pessimism or despair recede to intent, drive, desire.

When they come, such highs become more than therapeutic coping mechanisms, but serve as singular occasions for revelation and revelry: poetry in motion, motion as poetry, revolution in momentous reckoning. With everything to gain simply by getting out in the elements for a while, you'd think I'd do this running thing more often.

The runner's high can be elusive and unpredictable, and it's amusing to me that beginning runners often experience it the way many people try smoking marijuana: the first few times, nothing, and then . . . finally! You feel the sensation that everyone has been talking about, and you want to do it again and soon, preferably with others who are cool and who get it.

In time, you might find yourself smiling despite yourself during the final minutes of a run, no matter how short the distance. It is important to practice not clenching or tensing up on the shred; that goes for your jaw as much as your arms and legs, and you'll notice that a slight smile will encourage your entire face and the nape of your neck to relax. I find I'm still like many beginning runners who pre-emptively tense up before every workout—this is going to hurt!—as if I'm daring the run to surprise me or prove me wrong. I'm always recursively relearning how to open up to the possibility of joy, of childlike wildhood.

Also like clockwork, the sun has left the sunroom, and so I'm making sure the aromatherapy is going and mood lighting is on. Someone in the group is looking for a late-morning run tomorrow, and I might just take part. It's been too long seeking out the solitude of the long-distance runner. That's another thing about the runner's high: it's something you want to talk about and share.

The best runner's high typically comes after a long run or race. And though the urge to race, like the urge to travel, has been reduced to a dull ache—something I'd like to do in theory, but know I'm not going to do, at least not for the foreseeable future—it is still simmering inside me somewhere, deep in the furnace.

There are upcoming races in New Orleans (NOLA) with limited registration that I'm tempted to sign up for. As it happens, I'm even the defending champion of one of them, the Jackson Day Race, an historic 9K event that's been run for well over a century. I went down there in January to defend my title, but they ended up cautiously postponing the race due to possible hurricane weather which never materialized, then canceling it outright in March once COVID-19 took over. I don't think I'll make the trip this year, as I find it hard to imagine going all the way to NOLA, which turned out to be my last trip out of town, and keeping appropriate social distance. That's simply not the NOLA way. When I broke the tape last year, I had the biggest smile plastered on my face, and I couldn't keep myself from asking the guy handing me a bottle of water if I could hug him, even though I was undeniably sweaty and probably still retching a bit. Reader, he said yes. And then we laughed together.

Another thing about runner's high you might expect is that it doesn't last. But I swear that this one from New Orleans 2019 is ongoing. It is a pilot light burning in my furnace, emanating outward from me to you as we speak.

November 11, 2020

For the second day in a row, I get up and get outside in the morning. Today I even had time to make a smoothie before meeting up with three dudes at Beyond Running. Two of them, Chris and Caleb, ran that marathon in Detroit Lakes on Halloween, and then there was Josh and me. It turns out Josh and I have a lot in common, from the reasons we got into running to our predilection for sub-7:00 pace regardless of the workout. I realized how people like Josh and me rely on others to keep us from turning up the shred every single workout. Of course, our mate Adam typically logs more than eighty miles a week with an overall average in the area of 6:10 pace. That's some serious shredding, to be sure, but it can easily become unnecessarily draining, physically and mentally, as every workout metamorphoses into a tempo run.

This is what happens every time I get on the treadmill; I plan to run no faster than 7 flats but end up running between 38:30 and 39:30 for a 10K. The next day I plan to take it easy but still I find myself ramping it up to sub-6:30 by the end of a five-mile recovery run. Mostly, I just want to finish the workout, but a part of me also feels badass, treadmill becoming shredmill with each incremental increase in pace.

True to form, Josh and I started out slower, then clipped off a 6:47 halfway in, then a 6:35. Josh suggested we back off a bit, and just soak up the wayward high we had run ourselves into. We ended up running a bit under 7:02 pace for eight miles. Josh took third last year at the Dick Beardsley Half Marathon that Adam won (by five and a half minutes), achieving his goal of getting under 1:20 in the process. I was a mere minute ahead of him in 2019, but I'm not expecting that to last. I could see Josh knocking off some serious minutes should he decide to go there with the training.

I also see a kindred spirit in Josh, someone who loves and respects the running community we have here, but also someone who struggles with consistency and belief. He and I are already gearing up for a long, cold winter of sporadic training punctuated by no upcoming races. By contrast, Chris is going to run a marathon in the spring one way or another, and Caleb is going to do a half-Ironman triathlon next summer. They're recovering from a heroic effort of eleven days ago, a marathon whose course and conditions were decidedly less than ideal, but they're already planning for the next one. A few months ago, I had toyed with the idea of running the Rome Marathon again next spring, but I figure it'll eventually be canceled or postponed, just as Boston was recently. That leaves my shred card completely open.

Like a lot of Europe, Italy is currently reverting to lockdown mode, and as you should expect by now, I can't imagine "running" the Rome Marathon virtually here in Fargo, any more than I can imagine "eating" a virtual pizza from the best pizzeria in Rome. I only want to run races and eat pizzas without scare quotes. I wonder if European race organizers have floated such options by their staff, and whether such virtual races would even make sense to a Roman contingent in particular. Rome is admittedly not the most running-friendly city on the map, but you still would want to shut down its traffic for a few hours, wouldn't you? The only other surefire way to do that would be for Italy to win the World Cup again.

Since the 2019 Dick Beardsley Half, Josh and I have only run once together before today. Has it really been a whole year? I remember talking about Lonna's mom Beth and early-onset dementia with him, and today he asked me how she was doing. He says he thinks about her a lot since our last shred together, which means more than I could express to him. The truth is Beth's cognitive faculties have declined markedly since the pandemic and were already chumming the late stages coming into 2020. We are all atrophying to a greater or lesser degree these days, but of course it's no consolation for Lonna or me, as we see Beth recede into herself, scarcely responsive to the sound of our voices or faces on a Zoom meeting. It wasn't all that long ago that we could laugh together, walk around her facility, and sing along to the Beatles. We knew where the song was going, and where in turn to go.

Josh asking me and thinking about Beth, whom he's never met, is more than a consolation. It means the world. I am reminded and overwhelmed by how running can be a catalyst for empathy, how it—should we choose to go there—allows us to bring our most vulnerable and most giving selves to the shred. As we collectively reckon with the fragile future, I become less invested—meaning I couldn't care less about convincing you that I'm right. Instead, shredding is all about locking into the pace of empathy, which we set into motion by moving together through this superficially coldhearted world. We have embarked on an epic journey to discover the best version of ourselves; chumming the ocean of life, we move at the pace of empathy.

My return to running and Beth's dementia happened at more or less the same time. Both force you to relearn the intricate relationship between body and mind. People tend to approach both running and dementia (and body and mind, for that matter) through the lens of what can no longer be done, the general assumption being that it's more or less game over for ever getting in shape because "I'm not really a runner," or that the loved one with dementia is more or less checked out, basically just marking time until she can finally be at peace. None of it is true, but I understand why it is tempting to reckon it that way.

In the early days (2013–17), back when Bethy and I would go out for pizza and beer on the regular, I remember parking at the bottom of the hill by Rhombus Guys. I must have been talking about running, because Beth and I started to run together up the hill. We'd often walked to the café together, and once we even climbed the terribly steep dike by the Red River. But something about this run up the hill (cue Kate Bush) has stuck with me. I think it has something to do with the idea that Beth started it, that we were laughing the whole way, and that it seemed the most natural thing in the world for us to do.

Kate Bush's *Hounds of Love*, from 1985, has been one of my absolute favorite LPs ever since its release. I heard the opening track "Running Up That Hill" for the first time on the college radio station WNUR, out of Evanston, Illinois. Kate's hill may be more metaphorical than the one by Rhombus Guys, but I'm of the belief that everything in that song, like so much of Bethy's adored Beatles catalog, was hibernating for decades beneath the surface to reveal yet another layer of dynamic meaning to me today: "if I only could / I'd make a deal with God / and I'd get him to swap our places." Perhaps we swap places when we run. Perhaps we do more than share the road. Perhaps we share the same spirit, the same soul.

As for Beth and me,
there was thunder in
our hearts. We moved
at the pace of empathy.

November 12, 2020

Ellen Bass has a solid poem about the raging forest fires throughout the US in the most recent issue of *The Nation*. Built through matter-of-fact observations about her own displaced children ("They arrived at 3 AM"), the threatened neighborhood surroundings ("A man sleeps in his car, seat tilted back"), and up-to-the-minute briefings and wind reports ("Breeze is what we don't want"), the relatively unadorned poem "74,000 Acres of Forest Burning" creates tension through emotive restraint. Every moment of witness is set off from the others, such that each discrete observation is given equal footing. This almost listless listing compelling the poet—poetry as autonomic response to trauma, as linguistic survival instinct—culminates for me in this line: "An ant carries a broken ant across the patio." Macro not only connects to micro in this line, the reader intuits immediately that ants and humans have the same capacity for love, that our struggle for survival ultimately depends on making that reciprocal intersubjective I-You connection between humans, trees, and insects.

French novelist Bernard Werber has a series of novels specifically about the ant-human relationship, the first of which, *Les fourmis*, has been translated into English as *Empire of the Ants*. I admit it's been hard to do something about the anthills in my yard since teaching the book. We probably intuitively, instinctively, know that humanity's fate is intimately related to the bees, who pollinate most everything we eat, and whose numbers are declining rapidly. Yet their epic struggle is largely unsung, taken for granted. And while we're at it, what about the rats, bats, and wombats?

Bass's is not a poem about running, to be sure, but about our collective reckoning with imminent devastation, our helplessness before the raging forest fires, our inability to withstand the forces that promise more of the same—and, more than likely, much worse—year after year after year. We belong to the terrorized and the terrorists. But in the ant carrying its broken friend across the patio, I see myself—in both ants.

Running embodies a similar impulse, that our best selves can come out when we put ourselves out there on course. The marathon can be read as a collective reenactment of the epic struggle of survival, where the goal is to carry everyone across the finish line. The course is our pheromone trail, if you will, how we commune and communicate with each other, how we rely on each other to know where to go. I'm sure we look like ants to the birds.

It's warmer than it was around this time yesterday, but it feels colder. I'm sure this paradox makes perfect sense to you. If I don't suit up and brave the weather when it's in the 20s—but feels like 9°F!—I more than likely won't when it's actually in the single digits. It won't get above freezing today, so I better get used to it. Repeat today's mantra after me: I am the furnace churning at the pace of empathy. If that doesn't get me through three gray and dreary single-digit windchill miles, I don't know what will.

Just when you think
you know how the rest
of the day is going to
play out, the sun makes
a late-morning appearance
and changes the mental
landscape. Subtly, utterly,
an ant's life, a cat's, your own.

Then I hear Gracie, my furry nautilus of possibility, meowing for attention and treats, spot on time. She shall have both.

November 13, 2020

Another week comes to a close in the epicenter of the pandemic. I'm talking about Fargo, North Dakota, but also the United States, and France, India, Argentina as well, and . . . well, just about everywhere. Let's do some quick math: nationwide figures alone for coronavirus cases topped 140,000 the other day. That translates to 980,000—almost a million!—cases per week, a curve of such proportions that, unless flattened, could potentially reach more than 50 million infected per year, maybe one out of every six Americans? Right now, the numbers are headed in the wrong direction, in all senses. One week the newspaper obituaries feature a man in his late fifties who died of COVID-19, the next tells of a thirty-five-year-old who suffered the same fate.

The death of newspapers—and of independent presses—is also on my mind today. I read the obits in the *Fargo Forum*, which has gone down to a hard copy twice a week. Lonna worked there during the last recession, when the newspaper staff was cut in half, one of myriad reminders that downsizing and streamlining all sectors of the workforce was well underway before the pandemic. I don't know if I can handle doing the math regarding how many people have applied for unemployment, gone into bankruptcy, are homeless, have no healthcare, are suffering. How many acres of forest were lost, did you say? How many wombats in Australia?

Even if you're not otherwise a numbers person, as a runner you more than likely have invented ways to play games with time. You may cover up the treadmill data with a magazine, but you still want to know the numbers at the end. Even if you don't do Strava, you may obsessively—let's say avidly—check splits during and after a run. As mentioned, I get a kick out of *not* looking at my low-end Garmin until near the very end, then seeing how consistent I am with intuitively finding that pacing sweet spot run after run. I also like it when someone else intones the split we just did together—or relates them to me at the end. Then we are just playing games with time, recording the minutes of an epic and singular meeting of bodies and minds.

If I look at the clock and it's 2:43 p.m., I think about my marathon PR. If it's 2:52 p.m., then that's the time I'm going to run for my next marathon. At 5:30 p.m., I wonder how long I can still hold 5:30 pace, while remembering that I managed it for nine kilometers to win the Jackson Day Race last year. And truth be told, if the price at the pump happened to be $2.39, I'd fill up the tank and drive to the marathon starting line before I forget about the random portent of a sub-2:40 shred. If your mailbox reads "642," I'll pass by and think about how I ran 6:42 pace the other day, as well as for the entire 2018 Chicago Marathon.

I know I'm not alone in crunching the numbers, on the lookout for good omens. Dick Beardsley famously saw "209" (or "902") pop up in odd places on the way to Duluth, Minnesota, for Grandma's Marathon in 1981, and ended up setting the course record in 2:09:37. The numbers are so often against us, or seem completely out of our control, and accelerated culture replete with the imminent economic and environmental devastation alluded to above exacerbates the sensation that we are running against the clock—and out of time.

Curiously, actual running allows us to experiment with myriad paces, manifold senses of time. It allows us to connect our desired pace with the richness of every minute when body and mind aren't racing but pacing each other.

Additionally, addition becomes an ally. Errands turn into a visualization practice for future shredding. Even the three-digit CVC code on the back of my credit card is a desired pace. I have no illusions about upsetting the credit card industry's profiteering by reading another layer of meaning into a number that's been anonymously and randomly ascribed to me. This is just one way my running self allows me to not completely despair as I move through the omnipresent depredations of capitalism, the constant reminders that time is money, and it's running out.

Because everything up to and including the air we breathe can be owned, rationed, poisoned, and withheld, rereading and refiguring the small and desultory words and numbers of the world at large is vital to our survival. Running offers one path to reimagine the world in body and soul, a world otherwise imagined from the perspective of cars and endless traffic: "packed like lemmings into shiny metal boxes / contestants in a suicidal race," as Sting sings in "Synchronicity II." The tedium is the message.

Now I write to you at 2:58 in the afternoon, the time Chris Hass ran in Detroit Lakes for the homegrown Halloween Marathon. I've made the pizza dough for the weekend, as well as stocked up on what must surely be the last of the Oktoberfest, only feeling mildly guilty for not running a few miles beforehand. It turned out to be an almost autumnal kind of day out, too, blustery but sunny, with temps even hitting 40°F . . . and that's above zero!

My jaw has a mind of its own. It moves at the speed of blight, the rate of extinction. I still want a poem that travels at the speed of wombat. I want a poem that asks: who is the goddess of small things, who? Is it nobody, is it you? I'm trying to make an argument about what running and poetry can do at the same time. I want a world with fewer commas, more run-ons.

And then Small Press Distribution out of California delivers the goods in terms of world lit—look, Ma, no Amazon!—and I couldn't be more excited: bilingual editions of poetry from Columbia (Lucía Estrada) and Uruguay (Marosa di Giorgio), a French novelist (Pierre Senges) riffing on Kafka's notebooks—practically the day after I finished a book about the world history of one line in Kafka's most famous story "The Metamorphosis"—and a new edition of Henry Dumas's poems.

The cosmically talented Dumas was shot by an NYC transit cop in 1968 at the age of thirty-three, three and a half months before I was born on September 11. Eugene Redmond's introduction is entitled "Poet Henry Dumas: Distance Runner, Stabilizer, Distiller." I am seeing a half-century of life flash before my eyes, starting with a gunshot and ending with a knee on George Floyd's neck for eight minutes and forty-six seconds, a length of time I can't wrap my head around, or play a mental game with, or parse enough to make sense of. It must never be forgotten that the air we breathe can also be choked out of us. I run with the spirit of poet Big George in my lungs, and distance runner Henry Dumas in my heart.

Ditto

was a sixth-grade go-to word I used to
get in trouble with. I only ever wanted to

cut to the chase. *All my life*, in this case,
just meant the same damn thing. All my

face-saving techniques backfired when I
tried on that space-saving word to refer to

me in abbreviated terms. Then came *yet*.
Yet was some kind of leaf of tea or smoke I

was way too young to have sipped or toked
from yet. Even *and* was a plastic pinwheel

flower on a too-thin straw spinning in a pre-
emptive Asian carp wind. Sometimes I feel

like my *I* is a kind of Martian visiting my *me*
my whole life long. Keep in mind *ditto* kept me

from being more than the same damn thing
to my friends or to Mr. Gavin. Truth be told,

Mr. Gavin wasn't all that bad a guy when he
said *don't be smart* when I said *ditto*. I had tried

to use a new word on him, and the new word
bit back. Later on, he'd try to get me to try out

for track. Now I wonder why the same damn
thing often seems to happen in a once-in-a-

lifetime kind of situation. You see a swarm
of Asian carp jumping around the boat, and

the whole world comes up as one grand *Ditto*.
Now I live in Fargo, and that means I have to

have different go-to words. Every day I hike up
the rim of my volcanic mouth in my sleep and

cry out to all the carp of my long Asian life: *Stop!*
And every night I mine another long-lost word.

November 16, 2020

Henry Dumas lived for a while in East St. Louis, and also jammed with Sun Ra on occasion. He was our Linton Kwesi Johnson, the Jamaican-British poet who featured on a PJ Harvey record a few years ago. Dumas's biography presages and establishes a framework—an interpretive lens—for understanding the social unrest and racial injustice that defines life in America in the 21st century. From Dumas's East St. Louis, we can glimpse the segregated and heavily policed surveillance-state future of Ferguson, Missouri. At the biblically significant age of thirty-three, Dumas was shot and killed in New York City, six weeks after Martin Luther King Jr. was assassinated in Memphis.

> I look deep into
> the kaleidoscopic
> mirror of America
> and say "you know
> the rest." But I'm
> pretty sure this isn't
> even remotely true,
> not for me, nor for
> the mirror that
> knows me.

If you're born and raised in the Midwest—even in the Chicagoland area—it's quite likely you've internalized some version of the inferiority complex stemming from others believing your home is nothing but a desolate flyover zone. On days like this whole month, I look out the window and don't need much convincing regarding the desolate part.

I've always assumed that my friends from the South have a different legacy to contend with, but maybe it's not that all that different in the end. I mean, aren't "southern" cities like Louisville and Memphis also technically in the Midwest? Perhaps we can at least agree that many people from both coasts willfully or ignorantly misread the Midwest and South alike as uniformly redneck-y and Bible-thump-y. They've also grown up with their own internalized complexes, to be sure.

I note in passing that I have friends from small-town biblically inspired hamlets like Bethlehem, Pennsylvania, and coastal burbs in New Jersey as well as Topeka, Kansas, and Shreveport, Louisiana, and their upbringing doesn't seem to have played out in a markedly different fashion from my own. Of course, I met many of them in the heart of the heartland of Champaign–Urbana. We either didn't get into those elite coastal universities, or we didn't bother trying. In most ways, we were just passing through, living out an on-the-ground version of flying over the cornfields and dairylands of American academe. A temporary appointment to a remote outpost in the Deep Midwest. That's been pretty much my whole life up to now.

I reckon that continuing to unpack more ruminations about my personal experience will eventually get more and more about the Midwest overall wrong, and that a Midwestern elegy of sorts would ultimately paint over too broad a swath of diversity, much like a hillbilly elegy might. Nonetheless, I'm compelled to look back at those Midwestern moments, and tease out a countercultural narrative of possibility for running and writing—two elemental and elementary ways to begin crafting something along the lines of a self and a worldview.

It seems fitting that I discovered both the elementary nature of running and writing in elementary school, and that middle schools in the Midwest taught me about my discoveries almost after the fact, in fact. As with most things in life, I didn't come to understand what I was doing until I'd already been doing it—essentially, adolescent existentialism in a nutshell—not until sixth- and seventh-grade teachers clued me into the fact that I had just written a poem (thank you, Mr. Stagge, for this and more), and that that first Condell Distance Classic tee (red with white lettering and stick-figure runners) that I wore to school one day meant I could be competitive on the track, if I wanted to (thank you, Mr. Gavin).

I'm thinking too much about the ugly weather these days—another Midwestern predilection, to be sure. The weekend was so desolate and windy—albeit not nearly as cold as it looked or sounded from inside—that I started reminiscing about growing up reading random science fiction culled from my dad's stellar collection. At one point, the man had over 25,000 tomes, the majority of which had to have been science fiction and fantasy. We'll never really know.

Even after decades of trying to downsize, even after having 600 boxes of books schlepped away in his dying days before his very eyes by a literary executor, his widow Wilma is still paying through the roof for a couple of storage areas with the remaining vestiges of this once-hallowed library of the future. I think of the emperor's archivist in Andreas Eschbach's *The Carpet Makers*—which I doubt my dad ever read—and think how Dad would be completely happy combing the arcane and obsolete corners of a cosmic library for all eternity. I hope that's what he's doing, in fact, though I figure it's unlikely.

Robert Silverberg's 1964 novel *Time of the Deep Freeze* involves one of those ice-age treks that dissuaded me from leaving the sunless sunroom bunker this weekend. I haven't read it in at least forty years, but I know it's there, and have since experienced the kind of deep-seated and interminable cold depicted therein. It's hard for me to believe that Silverberg is still alive, so much a part of my late father's generation he seems to be, but of course, he wasn't yet thirty when *Time of the Deep Freeze* came out.

Then there is the final third of Ursula K. Le Guin's *The Left Hand of Darkness*, which I first read in grad school, long after I'd mistakenly thought I'd put my father's favorite genre—and long-distance running, for that matter—safely behind me, when protagonists Genly Ai and Estraven must cross a giant sheath of ice in order to avoid detection by the authorities. The first time through, this section seemed like a slog (apologies!) when compared to the political intrigue unfolding in the capital city.

But now I remember more than the cold and the *Into the Wild*-esque level of risk involved in the trek that Ursula Le Guin (RIP) lovingly and painstakingly describes, which is like "To Build a Fire" times hundreds of miles. Ai is Terran, and Estraven a genderless native of a distant planet—they only take on gendered attributes when experiencing "kemmer," but let's table that plot point until the time of the deep freeze—and they must do more than work together if they are to survive. They must share the same spirit, if you will. When you journey into the wild or through the desert or across the ice, the boundaries between beings become tenuous and permeable, as gender, race, and place come in second place to other, more otherworldly, concerns. Liminality, in-between-ness, metamorphosis, interspecific and reciprocal symbiosis—the elemental prerogative of otherness.

Growing up in the Chicagoland area, i.e., the burbs and exurbs, meant reading Ray Bradbury's *Dandelion Wine* in middle school as well. Bradbury was born in Waukegan, Illinois, not that far from where I grew up, and where my stepfather lived for a time. From Dad, I knew about Ray Bradbury already, having listened to his gripping stories on cassette in the car in grocery store parking lots across the North Shore—pretty much the same way I experienced Blondie's "Heart of Glass" around that same time, i.e., a long time ago in a parking lot far away. A couple months after Dad's passing, I read a copy of his *Strangers in the Universe*, a collection of short stories by Clifford Simak, a contemporary of Bradbury's and also a Midwesterner, as it happens.

The more I read science fiction, as well as literature from and about Sicily, the closer I seem to get to understanding the father from whom I spent much of my adult life estranged, and to whom the passionate desperation that fuels my search for meaning and purpose is undoubtedly indebted. The Midwest still feels as otherworldly and inhospitable as ever, and I wonder if I'd feel less estranged by the proverbial flat-as-a-pancake and gray-as-far-as-the-eye-can-see surroundings if I'd grown up in Portland, Oregon, or northern Norway. But searching literature for intelligent life in the universe goes hand in hand with becoming attuned to one's immediate surroundings—and realizing over and over what a strange and unfamiliar planet the everyday ordinary home world truly is. Or: the more straight-edged the center, the weirder the fringe, as Craig, a grad school friend from Alabama, used to say.

With Dad's preferred literary genre spurring me on, I started returning to my home planet and not recognizing it at a very young age. Certain runs can do that as well. They make you teem with an energy you forgot you had, such that home and hometown feel transformed—or revealed—in some elemental and extraordinary way, intricately and intimately more complex and beautiful than you ever thought possible. And yet you *did* know all this at some point. You've always known it, only now you've chosen to celebrate it.

I'm reckoning with a memory of Dad and me running—racing, though I'm pretty sure Dad let me win—down the length of the post office in Arlington Heights, Illinois. We were no doubt going to see if anything had showed up in his post-office box—remember those?—the way I'd accompany him on any other errand about town. It all seems rather eerily and idyllically Bradbury-esque when I write it out, to be completely honest. Did we make a habit of racing each other to the front of the post office, or was it just the one time? Does that even matter? How old was I? Does *that* even matter?

I haven't forgotten the feeling of exhilaration I felt the first time Dad and I made that mad dash, how natural it felt to rely on someone else to run longer, faster, more joyfully. Nor have I forgotten—not completely, anyway—how entities like the US Postal Service and local library colored my experience of growing up in the Midwest, how they put our humble hamlets on the proverbial map. Such civic and public buildings seemed inherent to the vitality of any town, and through the kaleidoscopically curious lens of childhood I took them to be everlasting, integral testaments to a thriving local community, ones that could always be returned to.

Come to think about it, I even started writing my first real paper for grad school in the Libertyville Public Library over Thanksgiving Break in 1992, the initial draft composed with pen on notebook. I'd spent that first semester completely blocked, unable to concentrate. It was now or never, else my professors figure me for the complete fraud I felt like. I called that monster "In Pursuit of the Psychoanalytic Palimpsest," which sounds appropriately pretentious and unwieldy, typical of the first-year comparative literature graduate student. But writing this now reminds me that I'm still pursuing this goal. I'm still running and writing toward a symbiotic and manifold sense of belonging, an intricate kind of thrive mind.

I think about the otherworldly, science-fiction-y nature of both entities: the USPS antedates the US government, after all, and espouses the idea of sending and receiving messages from anywhere in the world, a dynamic and cosmic conversation coursing to and from the satellite of your home, following the orbit of empathy. Libraries are time-travel spaceships where any destination is imaginable, and all universes are possible—even a universe we feel at home in, yes, even that one.

November 17, 2020

I had to promise myself I would get my run in first thing this morning, else I make the coffee, sit down to the computer, and write myself into a comfy corner in the sunroom, ultimately neglecting our daily shred. Give us this day our daily shred . . . maybe a Runner's Prayer every morning would get me out the door more regularly. This is a non-denominational book I'm writing, but I don't bristle at the idea of running as a form of prayer and exercise of faith, part of an essential belief system and survival mechanism in a desecrated and devastated world. I wonder what would have happened if Søren Kierkegaard had regularly laced up the running shoes while writing *Fear and Trembling* or *The Sickness unto Death*.

To be clear, I'm not speculating that running offers access to some divine being in human form, but I see a similar kind of movement in running with Kierkegaard's subject who moves toward a god that moves farther away. Runners internalize the notion that the finish line is just another starting line. We may spend our entire lives moving toward something ethereal and elusive, something luminous always in the distance, a cosmic rabbit we'll never catch. With this sacred and dynamic movement, we harness the best versions of ourselves, the radiant being that has always been there, hibernating, waiting to be set into motion.

Of course, writing about running as a spiritual practice can be hard for me to reconcile with the unavoidable and blasphemously prolific tears, phlegm, and snot that always threaten to compromise the reverie. Dear reader, I even gross myself out. But ultimately what persists is a feeling of moving toward, fear and trembling giving way to a kind of humming, vibrating curiosity. What if I go this way instead? What if I add on another mile? What are the odds of someone playing "Amazing Grace" on the bagpipes midway through my birthday run? See, I haven't forgotten everything!

I'd taken five whole days off the shred, so today I ran five miles at just under 7:03 pace. I checked my phone for the temperature before going out, and it read: 14°F, feels like 7°F. Even now it sounds cold to me, colder than the last few days I opted to stay inside and watch some international soccer fixtures instead. But it truly wasn't; "feels like single digits (above zero)" is something you can totally dress appropriately for. I made a mental note to myself that I have a couple more protective layer options available to me once temps drop another twenty degrees or more. I didn't have to pull out all the sartorial stops, as it were, and by three-quarters of a mile I was warmed up and firing on all cylinders.

As usual, I thought to myself: hey, I should do this more often! I love stretching post-run and seeing the steam rise from my body, proof that the furnace is in working order. Then after a shower, I acknowledge that this is probably the best I'm going to feel all day. I just want to bask in the afterglow of our daily shred. And to top the morning off, my cakey-sweet cat Gracie is game for a little chase-and-pet herself, so I delay making the coffee in order to make myself available for one of our cutest, most classic rituals, which resolves to a quick catnap under the covers. We may look to dogs to rediscover the inherent joys of running, but cats have cornered the mental market on being in the zone.

> Body emanating heat
> I close my eyes
> a few more sighs
> with Cakey Sweet

It's not Emily Dickinson, to be sure, but it's a start.

The other cat, Woodman, aka Cap'n FOMO, must know that I'm writing about Gracie because he's compelled me to move the computer to the armrest so he can lock in on some lap time. (Why do we call them laps? I wonder). It's the cutest thing. The cat who came with the dementia, the somehow-broken-from-the-get-go Big Man of Wood, the oversized tom who attacks everyone, is really the softest of softies on the inside. Perhaps it's his little meow that gives the game away. Who is Woodman when he's not afraid?

Here's something to try: find and watch a clip filmed someplace you love from a year ago. Remind yourself what it's like to not freak out about sharing the same airspace with a stranger, and what a singular gift moving of one's own accord through the strange and beautiful world truly is. Yesterday, for example, I watched vlogger-runners Seth James DeMoor and Mike Kofuzi meet in person for the first time in Chicago—my old stomping grounds—in the summer of 2019. As they run along Lake Michigan, with the inimitable and singular Chicago skyline in the background of their GoPro cameras, I see them running toward the light beyond the camera eye, unbridled smiles on their faces.

They run past beaches I frequented in the mid-'80s, as well as in the vicinity of races I ran both in the early '80s *and* six or seven years ago. Somewhere nearby is a church where my parents got married, a couple years before I came into the story, and over there, just out of frame . . . well, you get the idea. So many palimpsests, so little time.

Farther on is Loyola University where my folks met, and beyond that is where Mom used to take us for bike rides and ice cream. If you keep heading north along the North Shore, eventually you'll get to Waukegan, birthplace of the aforementioned literary home-state hero Ray Bradbury.

Waukegan is also the site of the beach where Mom told me to run as far as I could, and for some reason I took her words at face value. I must have surely trespassed on private property, probably of some nuclear facility, before I turned around, the hours of the afternoon having just slipped away from me, my aching legs seizing up while seeing the Chicago skyline in the distance, then finally running into the arms of my crying mother, who by then was completely distraught from me going missing. Like finishing a marathon, like starting to yearn for something deeper and more epic.

Something altogether
more than imagined
possible heretofore . . .

Object Trajectory

I am thinking about how many tons of metal
and gallons of petrol it takes to take a person
across town versus how many miles a person
must walk across a desert before she can be said

to be safe. I am thinking about how many places
said person might drive or walk or bike to versus
how all the other species go where they go to and
whether they go by crawling, slithering, or flying or

otherwise. I am thinking about the word "rescue"
in fact and what it means in discrete contexts as in
19 cats were "rescued" from a North Fargo home
where their owner was said to be found sleeping on

a dirty mattress under his truck versus various reasons
were given for why police were initially prevented
from coming to the "rescue" of stunned citizens on
the island of Utoya just outside Oslo. Sometimes I

think about how all of this pertinent information
works its way through us and the end result is that
I think I should be thanking my lucky stars I made it
to the sucky weekend. I can think about the dog trainer

in Kentucky wanting to adopt two of the "rescued"
cats and the relative costs of taking said cats across
the Midwest versus say "adopting" an African child
or fixing said kid's cleft palate or say taking a Somali

family across the desert where "rescue" operations
are said to be underway despite being hindered by
various so-called insurgent factions. I am thinking
about the armed and dangerous world and all of

the valid arguments against leaving the comfy chair.
What's more, my horoscope today is a mere two-star
affair and even says "vanish while you can." I shit
you not. I am thinking long and hard about how to

take such advice. I think I get what reading between
the lines gets you and yet that's pretty much what I'm
all about. It's getting too dangerous to be thinking too
hard while taking the long view has gone the way of

the dinosaurs, more or less. Even five years down
the road sounds like more hard travel. Five years
down the road sounds like a kind of vanishing while
we can before said dinosaurs come to our "rescue."

November 19, 2020

After much hemming and hawing, as well as running out of excuses to *not* go running—I was aiming for something more legit than "I just didn't feel like it"—I went out for four miles at a 7:03 pace, pretty much within the couple-second margin of error of yesterday, the day before that, and a week ago yesterday with Josh. Sevens and change must be my windy, gray-day pace, even if I were to tell myself to do eights or nines.

Regarding my default running setting: I'm more likely to not run than cough up a couple miles on a cold, dreary day, no matter how easy I tell myself I can go, and even if it's the only time I'm going to leave the house that particular day. How messed up is that, right? I remember the Ray Bradbury story about a group of students locking a girl inside a school locker on the one day in seven years that the sun comes out on Mars—or Venus, I may be getting a couple details wrong here, but you get the gist. Once the rain starts back up, she is set free, but of course has to wait another seven years for the sun to reappear.

Arguably, a fair-weather runner is no runner at all; at least, that's what I tell myself to guilt-trip me into doing what's best for me. As a young child who looked forward to recess regardless of the weather—or so I recall—I thought about how horrible being kept from that one sunny day would have been, and how Ray Bradbury must have intimately understood how cruel my middle school peers could truly be. Right now, I'm thinking that one sunny day a week, much less one every seven years, might not be enough to get me through. All of which is another way of saying that if you or little orphan Annie can't promise me the sun will come out tomorrow, or next week, or next month, then you might as well keep your forthcoming hopeful sunny days to yourself.

As I'm heading out, Lonna shows me a video clip of Dan Jaworski, an ultramarathoner my age who has early-onset dementia, someone clearly in the early stages of his diagnosis. I recognize the smile and the enthusiasm—not to beat dementia per se, because no one does, no one has—but the desire to fight against both despair and the inevitable future, to live as full a life as possible despite the nonspecific but always imminent and looming death sentence of a dementia diagnosis.

Not to parse tragedies, mind you, but this is categorically different than reckoning with a cancer diagnosis. Dementia means giving up your most cherished memories, down to the names of your spouse and children, and then—inevitably, inexorably—your own. A dementia diagnosis means reading the rest of your life through the lens of oblivion. Oblivion on the installment plan.

So when I catch a glimpse on a phone of a fifty-two-year-old warrior on a stationary bike declaring his intent to shred dementia and never give in, I quit my own private pandemic pity party and get out there to run toward a greater awareness, a keener mindfulness, and a superior vantage point to reckon with and combat the suffering afflicting so many of us in the age of pandemic. By a half mile in, already the stakes have changed.

This morning I saw Beth via Zoom for the first time in a few weeks, and savored the brief smile that would flit across her face, her almost-imperceptible moment of recognition of the low register of my once-familiar voice, just her being in her world in the frame of my computer for twenty minutes, which is roughly the length of time it takes to get some perspective through movement. Movement: the call and response of the cosmos.

Because to be truly honest, I've been feeling like we're all doomed—certainly more than I've been feeling like help is on the way—and that the suffering is going to increase in the months and years to come. I'm not even going to bother with the idea of weeks here. But even government can change its mind and decide to help its people in a time of crisis, a vaccine for coronavirus could be just around the corner, and even a cure for dementia is not out of the realm of possibility. That said, if we continue to refuse to address the seriousness of climate catastrophe, these as-of-now-nonexistent palliatives may be short-lived indeed.

But what if I told you that I have an idea for a post-capitalist form of social organization that would eventually cure dementia, all while localizing and diversifying the economy, one built on environmental sustainability and community engagement to boot? This could totally happen, but I must warn you: there would be little appeal to being a billionaire in such a scenario—even millionaires would be rather funny specimens in this world—but perhaps a couple of them could pitch in at story time while we work through the Charles Dickens catalog for posterity.

What if such late-stage capitalists had to go door to door to make their case for making insane amounts of money because everyone else was busy making sure everyone else was taken care of? A genteel woman with a beautiful smile answers the door, and, though she refuses the pyramid scheme, Beth ends up inviting the billionaire in for a spot of tea. And, my fellow Americans, it so happens that the billionaire has rung at a fortuitous moment: there is fresh bread right out of the oven, made with all locally sourced ingredients. True story.

I'm telling you, my line of thinking may get even more outlandish once I get outside, but it's way more fun than staying indoors waiting for the proverbial hammer to fall (cue Queen). This is what I think about when I think about shredding: how to save the planet and myself in the bargain. Twenty or thirty minutes later, and I want to stick around long enough to see how things turn out. I reach out to the suffering many, our dying planet. I outrun the proverbial loneliness of my species.

Such reckoning means confessing a persistent fragility, a lifelong despair, a profound ineptitude, and a deep-seated fear for the future. By the way, why don't we say "deep-seeded," as the expression refers to that which we sow deep within us, and which takes root within the very core of our being?

For now, I'm going to imagine that you exist until I learn you do. I'm writing and running toward the parallel universe in which we all survive extinction and end up living in a kind of chaotic harmony with too many kinds of seeds to name. Paraphrasing Carrie Brownstein of Sleater-Kinney, the stakes should be high. Anything that smacks of settling for less isn't worth putting on paper.

November 23, 2020

We are taught to be realistic before we learn about the quote-unquote real world. We learn to temper our expectations before we know what it means to expect something, to ardently work toward something bigger than reality, to hope for and believe in the revolutionary heart and soul required to move beyond the real. In America, especially, you may find yourself at the end of a campaign with a striking paucity of options in terms of leadership, though the recent Democratic primary functioned quite like the cereal or soft-drink aisle of the supermarket: offering the illusion of choosing between myriad candidates, all of whom are beholden to General Mills or Coca-Cola. Note that I eschew the antediluvian locution of "grocery store" in favor of a term that reminds us how everything, from the food we eat to and the water we drink to the government we elect, exists in one behemoth, superlative market. By the way, RIP the refreshing diet soda alternative that was Tab.

As I sift my way through the marketplace of ideas from the comfort of the hand-me-down sofa in the sunroom bunker on another Monday in the age of pandemic, relishing the sunlight that has come some 93 million miles to remind me that reality hinges on a certain slant of light (Dickinson, as well as the name of my bygone high school literary journal), I'm aware and wary of the compulsion to brand myself, to trademark shredding as the latest market-driven initiative for self-improvement. I'm always-already trying to be realistic about being idealistic. I'm always-already worried that the desire to outrun capitalism is perhaps created by the marketplace itself, the toxic status quo rebranded as a nominally healthier alternative to business as usual. Tell that to the polar bears in the Arctic, who don't discern the difference between Democrat and Republican drilling initiatives, or the babies in Yemen, or the refugees on the border of everywhere.

After a couple days off, I went out for 5.5 miles at a 7:04 pace, and the sun even showed up for the majority of the run. I could probably just make up the pace and distance of the next runs from here on out, and no one would be the wiser. That said, runners—obsessed as we are with workouts and races—wouldn't make up a time or distance, the watch acting as a benevolent surveillance system that presides over and offers praise for all shredworthy endeavors, a data-fueled panopticon for the wrist. We want the technology's numerical affirmation that we came, we saw, we shredded.

Since the infamous Rosie Ruiz crossed the Boston Marathon finish line and was crowned the winner in 1980, there have been periodic attempts at faking victory, and to the runner in me they read like the strangest of pathologies. Why would anyone ever want to claim a time and title that isn't genuine? On the smaller race circuits, many cuttings of corners are no doubt left undetected—and are often unintentional—especially if you have a race director hell-bent on providing the ideal race experience for everyone, offering a half-dozen events around the same time, and/or making courses exceedingly convoluted, with turns and turnarounds aplenty. Here in Fargo, I've seen leaders go off course in the first mile of a confusing 5K, or middle-of-the-packers pack it in a few miles before running the full 26.2. They could even cross the finish line and everything, if they were of a mind to.

And of course, performance-enhancing substances have become part and parcel of late-stage capitalism's athletics arena and should be expected by a culture that defines success by absurd profit margins and killing the competition. The surveillance technocracy goes hand in hand with Big Pharma and the addiction to endless war. We all know about Lance Armstrong's downfall, but the pressures to game the system affect athletes in all sports. Thirty-four years after Rosie Ruiz faked winning Boston, Rita Jeptoo was forced to relinquish her Boston 2014 title, the year after the bombing and the year Meb Keflezighi won the men's race. We know Jeptoo ran the entire race, at least, and that even her undeniable natural talent didn't prevent her from caving in to the pressure to cross a performance-enhancing (and career-ending) line.

I was surprised to learn that Rosie Ruiz passed away last year, on July 8, 2019. She was sixty-six. Born in 1953, the first year of the Cuban Revolution, Ruiz came to America from Cuba at the age of eight, having to leave her father behind. I'm suddenly wide-eyed by stray details: didn't finish college, had three kids, faked her performance at NYC in 1979 before the following year's Boston, died of cancer in Florida, is survived by a female life partner.

When you think about it, Ruiz's life trajectory isn't all that different from Alberto Salazar's, whose father was directly involved in the Cuban Revolution, a friend of Fidel Castro's before Castro decided to ban religion. Unlike Ruiz's father, Salazar's moved with the family to America. Alberto grew up in a hardworking, devout household, and was for a time the greatest marathoner who ever lived. He is also currently serving a four-year ban on coaching due to a history of questionable behavior at the now-defunct Nike Oregon Project.

Growing up, I was a huge Bill Rodgers fan. Salazar, not so much. But only today, forty years later, can I see Rosie Ruiz and Alberto Salazar as two sides of the same Cuban American coin, a currency indiscernible from American capital. How do we define achievement in this country, if not by the requisite by any means necessary gumption and persistence to be number one? My dad faked a few things in his life, to be sure, but I forgive him for his trespasses. Incidentally, my dad's widow Wilma was born (in the Philippines) the same year as Rosie Ruiz.

I recall being indignant, if not outraged, by Rosie Ruiz the first time around. But for what it's worth, I feel differently today. Much of the controversy around Salazar derives from his alleged treatment of women, the testimony of which seems—to this runner—to be quite damning. I read his book *14 Seconds* when it came out, and it's stuck with me. But, from one lapsed Catholic to a devout one, I'm in no position to offer absolution.

Here we might have to pivot to the whole question of ghostwriting, the status quo of political speeches and memoirs alike—also typical for sports or music autobiographies—the inevitable excessive borrowing that occurs in the cut-and-paste world of contemporary media, such that politicians might even come to think they are writing a speech or a memoir, when they are in fact simply spit-balling ideas online with a trained professional (former Minnesota governor and short-lived presidential hopeful Tim Pawlenty comes to mind). From here on out, know that these longwinded tweets I send you are my own, my whole truth, and nothing but.

November 25, 2020

After writing a couple of days ago, I decided to celebrate the arbitrary milestone—an appropriate and wonderful word—of reaching 35,000 words in this extended rumination on running and being with a 3.5 mile run at a 7:06 pace. I told myself to go as slowly as possible while contemplating the intertwined and elemental nature of writing and running. There is no real finish line ahead, no imagined end product; there is the elemental movement of body and mind across planet and page, and that is enough.

More dedicated runners than I would no doubt have run 35K, i.e., 21.7 miles, to celebrate reaching 35K words. And from writing this fall, I've gotten the sneaky feeling that every mile is worth at least a thousand words. Does this mean that every kilometer is worth roughly two-thirds of that length? No, grasshopper. Every kilometer is worth at least a thousand words as well.

The eternal halving movement of Zeno's paradox might come into play after a while. For all I know, I might start cutting the distance of thought in half until it takes me a thousand words to describe getting out the door. Perhaps I already halve! I'm writing a thousand-word haiku with every epic stride, keeping in mind the fact that entire books have been written about a single long jump: namely, Bob Beamon's "perfect" jump at the 1968 Olympics in Mexico City. The year of my birth was a year when revolution and counterrevolution were in the streets, the entire world at war—and in many ways a war that is ongoing. Since reading historian and novelist Paco Ignacio Taibo II's short memoir about the protests in Mexico City in 1968 a few years back, I have slowly and sporadically started to piece together more of the global context informing Beamon's unanticipated giant leap for humankind.

The 1968 Olympics also featured the three 200-meter medalists Tommie Smith, Peter Norman, and John Carlos raising their fists—the Black Power salute—in solidarity with African Americans: Colin Kaepernick and Black Lives Matter *avant la lettre*, and a testament to the intricate intersections of global sport and politics. Smith and Carlos are African American, but Norman was Australian (he died in 2006) and white. His career was effectively ended by this one gesture—also about which entire books have been written—despite the fact that he is undeniably Australia's greatest 200-meter runner. His time at the 1968 Olympics, 20.06 seconds, still stands as their national record for the distance.

I write "despite," but part of me wonders if I should have written "because of" instead. Maybe power needs a platform—or a podium—to make the powers that be take notice. If you only sell a few thousand copies of your book, or have a few thousand subscribers to your vlog, no big deal. It's when the depredations and hypocrisies of power are laid bare on the national and world stage for all to see that the powerful feel threatened, their surveillance system suddenly turned back on itself. Rather than assume that no one really cares about what I write or assert, however, I must teach myself to become attuned to the immanent power of a single gesture, a single jump, or a haiku-length afterthought.

In time, the footfalls
of a run become
their own mantra,
metric feet probing for
staccato isometric insight.

Though Peter Norman's story is tragic in many ways, he will go down in history as a hero, a champion of human rights whose single gesture created a global solidarity that wasn't there before. Running happened to create the context for this moment, but if we allow ourselves to warm up to the idea, we can feel the energy of solidarity in the simplest movements. It may take 35,000 words or thirty-five kilometers, but solidarity lies in wait for our mutual vulnerability, our reciprocal openness to being each other's salvation. (Is solidarity a secular form of salvation? Discuss.) I think about bonking around 35K of the New York City 2017 marathon, and reaching my left arm out to fellow sufferers, urging them to help me get home. And, eventually, we did.

At around twenty miles, I was walking while vocally declaring that this was my last marathon ever, in the throes of that "here we fail again" shadow consciousness that defines the proverbial Wall. But when I reached out my hand to encourage someone else, I felt immediately better, almost blessed for being there to help out. Someone else even passed me while praising my "good sportsmanship." One day I hope to return to that momentous milestone of the NYC marathon and reckon with it better.

There are moments in a marathon where clichés or figures of speech return to their elemental and unadulterated beauty, the jaded and "adult" approach to language superseded by the childish glee and revelation inherent in the idea of poetry in motion. The truism that "we're all in this together" is one of those, as is "poetry in motion." If uttered with the reverence of a youngster just coming into language, I might even champion that otherwise-loathed neologism "it is what it is." Because the child will always put an exclamation point at the end.

November 27, 2020

This morning I ran four miles at a 7:03 pace, the raw temperature outside inching toward 20°F, the sun making the run invigorating rather than bleak. Heading west, I watched my tall shadow stretch in front of me, and heading back over the 12th Avenue bridge, I had to squint and look askance, half-blinded by the sun, eyes tearing up, furnace churning into the wind, that strange combination of relaxation and resistance as I mindfully recalibrate my stride to suit the ever-shifting terrain and trajectory of shred.

Even a basic four-mile run involves myriad accelerations and adjustments which go largely undetected by the watch and unrecorded in the running log. The fact that my average pace always ends up being more or less the same bemuses me, if only because the experience of each run seems predicated on the notion of singularity. What can I observe in the next half hour or so? What will I think about? How can I use running as a force for good?

And yet, I'm also paradoxically using the half hour to clear my head, and flush out the draining tensions of the multi-tech life on this couch. If you've been feeling depleted this pandemic, tired and depressed without knowing why, overly irritable and anxious, and perhaps utterly pissed off at everyone and everything on occasion, then our default settings have a lot in common.

As a lifelong sufferer of depression, I can tell you that I've never wanted to end it all after a run, and I feel immediately less debilitated by fear of the future. Only after the news—of endless wars and interminable food lines, of record-breaking infections and death tolls, of melting icecaps and burning forests—do I remember to remember that we're doomed. In addition, the real-time newsreel of the middle of the night doesn't offer much hope or solace, either. No rest for the wicked, as Dad used to say, no sleep of the just. But perhaps one of those purring furnaces might happen by, and model for me how to keep the pace of good sleep.

Because I'm not doing mega-mileage, that half hour ends up having more at stake in some respects; it is hallowed *because* of its brevity. I don't have time to feel compelled to tune out the first few miles, say, or that first hour of a long run. True, it feels like I'm just loosening up, just getting to that feeling of being dialed in to a given pace, only running to the very beginning of the endorphin rush. I know that when I decide to go longer, there will be more endorphins and more insight.

Looking back on the last sporadic three months, my predictable four- or five-mile runs don't feel like a rut, or even a holding pattern anymore—at least not any more than a pandemic is one or the other. The shred—that singular, harmonic, revelatory, elemental, and dynamic ideal—is often the only time I'm outside on any given day, and sometimes the only time I leave the house at all. Still, writing and reflecting on running and being this fall is incrementally changing something within me; it is opening up a cosmic portal, a wormhole of possibility that compels me to reverse the polarity on my pessimistic worldview. I thought I'd strayed off-course—the nightmare of every runner—but I was wrong. I just had to reverse the polarity.

Granted, I was down for the count (another Dad-ism) by seven p.m. yesterday, but this morning I even did a load of laundry and ran a couple errands after the run, including procuring a few bottles of specialty beer from Junkyard and picking up another pair of running shoes at Beyond Running. The sun stayed out the whole time, too! Cody took care of me at the Junkyard, and Sally and Jake were both at the downtown store to greet me. I don't need to tell Jake my shoe size, or even which color I'd prefer, for that matter.

My previous pair of the Brooks Ghost were gray and black because that's all they had in size nine. I must say that I quite like the purple-blue hue of this new pair—classy! Seriously, I could see myself in a three-piece pinstripe suit with this color scheme. From behind the mask, I told Jake and Sally that I missed them, and that I'd think of them whenever I put this new pair on my feet. It's really an easy, natural promise to keep in the end.

I currently have five different pairs of shoes in the running room from five different companies. In alphabetical order by make: Adidas Boston 9, Asics Evoride, Brooks Ghost, Enda Lapatet, and Saucony Endorphin Speed. Brooks have been go-to shoes for me for some time, but I like to try out rides other than the tried and true. I've also run in Hoka, New Balance, Nike, Mizuno, and Pearl Izumi since the running reboot of 2012. I suppose you could say that this entry is unilaterally unsponsored, but multilaterally shredicated, to boldly go where my feet and mind take me, a force for good grinding it out one footstrike at a time.

American Childhood

I never outkicked anyone,
except for this one time
during the eighth-grade half

at the high school track,
when in the final stretch
I took the lead and crossed

the line like Prefontaine—
I believe I clocked a 2:29—
and thought I could see

my grandpa cheering me
on from the stands, exactly
the way he might root

for the horses he bet on,
a desperate Sicilian who
can hardly believe he's won,

and who afterwards gushed
in proud disbelief that I'd
destroyed my unsuspecting

peers, as if with this measly
victory all of the diaspora
might yet be saved. Anyone,

especially me, was down for
such a yarn. I was a kid
who'd do just about anything

to save some face or please
someone else. I didn't realize
until several lifetimes later

that, in running as in life,
you are mostly competing
against yourself. And though

Grandpa never attended
another meet, and though
I never outkicked anyone ever

again, I made sure to keep
my desultory pursuers at bay.
I always made sure I made

enough of a statement at
the outset that the thought
of reeling me in was to meet

the ancient ire of his stare,
watching his "half-dago" grandson,
who broke the tape and won.

SHRED!

November 30, 2020

The last day of the month, and it feels like I should have something to show for it. I'd have to look back at what I've written to see what exactly I've accomplished, if anything, or if I've had any breakthroughs. I have to retrace my steps to remember my elemental place in the universe.

My friend Matt from Champaign–Urbana just underwent an emergency surgery the week before Thanksgiving, and I was reminded of all our late-night listening sessions, breaking down riff after riff of every song, assessing the risks and merits of every song's move, production value, and pace. Both aspiring songwriters and guitarists who met up in grad school, we brought the same kind of geeked-out critical acumen to rock as we did to literary criticism. He bought me the latest Ween CD (*Chocolate and Cheese*) back in the day when I had mono and had to bail on my band Nastybake's first gig, which would have been a house party at Matt's in Urbana in late 1994 or early 1995.

The previous year, I'd organized a conference on rock and critical theory with Jonathan Sterne, bass player of Nastybake, and currently shredding a Professorship of Cultural Studies at McGill University in Montreal, Quebec. Though his advisor, Larry Grossberg, was initially skeptical of Jonathan working with a comparative literature student on the event—lest I overly privilege the lyrics as primary text, I suppose—we pulled it off, and had a fine time meeting other like-minded rock-and-theory geeks. And Nastybake's in-the-near-future drummer-in-waiting, prof and critic Michael Bérubé, also attended the proceedings. At the very least, we did our small part in creating this postmodern hybrid; I'm just saying the credit shouldn't all go to Greil Marcus. For the record (ha!), I wholeheartedly enjoy musical biographies and journalism, including the 33 ⅓ series (from Bloomsbury Publishing), which delves into all the musical and theoretical particulars of a particular artist's particular record.

Looking back, those were weird days for music, an era of slippages and transgressions, and also one of capitalist cooptation. As canon and culture debates fueled the critical landscape, indie bands were being picked up by the majors, who would then drop them at the drop of a high hat. For a brief period in the mid '90s, Champaign was believed to be "the next Seattle," or at least the industry was making a decided investment in such an idea. Ultimately, lives were ruined; rock and roll suffered.

Members of Babes in Toyland, Rage Against the Machine, and Tool attended Libertyville High School (LHS), as did Marlon Brando for a time, though he didn't graduate. Rage's Tom Morello's mom taught at LHS and was instrumental (sorry) in organizing a pro-music response to Tipper Gore's infamous Parents Music Resource Center (PMRC). As it happened, Jonathan's paper for the Rock in Theory Conference explored the contradiction between the Gores' desire to police transgressive forms of music and their love of dancing to the suggestive grooves of James Brown.

At the University of Illinois Urbana-Champaign, you'd hear frat bars and sororities playing Jane's Addiction and The Cult. I was outside the monthly Criticism and Interpretive Theory lecture when Tony Kirschner of the band Free Range Chicken informed me that Kurt Cobain had taken his own life. Tony had presented at the Rock in Theory conference as well. I ended up dedicating my dissertation to David Williams, a friend from the program who took his own life around this time. I'm not sure how much I truly understood about the momentous nature of the '90s musical and cultural Zeitgeist as it happened, but they were heady times indeed.

I always used to get down on myself for mistakes I made on stage, which, like string breaks, were low-hanging fruit for me—except that most people didn't notice most of them most of the time, or the fuckup turned into a happy accident that signified the singularity of the occasion. I feel like I spent most of the conference stressing about it, all the while worrying about the minor lapses in my composure or ability to articulate a cogent response. It was a strange kind of fun indeed to always fall short of the illusory gold standard I'd set for myself or the band. Being hyperconscious—the lot of the critical theorist and self-deprecating grad student alike—means the moments of being in the moment come few and far between. And yet a sense of belonging, of common purpose, is what I hold onto most about grad school at UIUC.

At the very least, I can tell you this: twenty-five years is next to nothing.

I didn't run yesterday, but I watched Napoli beat Roma four-nil on the computer. The entire soccer world is currently mourning the loss of Diego Armando Maradona, the Argentinian striker, quite possibly the greatest footballer of all time, who died at the age of sixty. Like Eddie Van Halen, Maradona was one of a kind; both maestros were famously mercurial and quixotic off the pitch or the stage, but completely at home in the world with a ball on the feet or guitar in the hands.

Think of EVH's impish grin, the childlike glee involved in inventing new ways to make a guitar sound. Before the age of social media, Maradona was both king and court jester, as feared for his prowess on the pitch as adored for his entertaining warmups. Hailing from a shantytown in Buenos Aires, Maradona turned his hardscrabble life into an international rags-to-riches bildungsroman for impoverished aspiring athletes—especially those who are of literal shorter stature. You can see it in his compatriot Lionel Messi, as well as the elite tennis player Diego Schwartzman. Born in Argentina in 1992, Schwartzman is one of many—I wonder how many, actually—kids in the '80s and '90s to be named after the man who led Argentina to World Cup victory in 1986. I mean, the leader of Argentina declared that there be three days of national mourning last week for Diego Maradona.

Maradona famously joined Napoli in the '80s, then a fledgling *calcio* team at best, and led them to two Serie A titles by 1990. Soon they're going to rename the stadium for him. And just as it is fitting that Messi scored in Barça's four-nil defeat over Osasuna yesterday (Maradona also played for Barcelona for a spell), it was wonderful to see Napoli's short and dynamic Lorenzo Insigne open the scoring from a set piece in Napoli's all-but-empty home stadium, their first home match since Maradona had passed. Both Messi and Insigne looked to the heavens in their goal celebrations, and Insigne kissed a special edition number 10 jersey on the sidelines as well.

My Sicilian grandparents were also very short, and it meant something to them that Dad was taller than they were, and that I was getting to be taller than Dad. Maybe the logic has to do with moving up in the world: if your genes can do it, then certainly the rest will follow. Indeed, the shorter you are in most sports, the harder you have to work for it, not just in the obvious case of basketball, but also in tennis, soccer, and running. Diego Schwartzman gets no free points off his serve, a Messi header is harder to come by than one by Olivier Giroud (6'4"), and the great Kenyan marathoner Eliud Kipchoge is also a mere five and a half feet tall.

My search to verify this statistic reminds me that two other distance greats, Ethiopia's Kenenisa Bekele and Uganda's Joshua Cheptegei, are 5'5" and 5'6", respectively. Meb Keflezighi is 5'5", as is Shalane Flanagan. Deena Kastor is 5'4". Maybe being short of stature means being compelled to cultivate the tenacity to excel in one's sport of choice. In running terms, size doesn't matter; it's all about turnover.

Grandpa Carollo died in 1986, but I also keep in mind Grandma Carollo's advice in the '90s to drop the "o" from my last name so I could publish something of significance. I wonder if you ever truly leave the ghetto of the mind and arrive at the proverbial promised land of freedom. Maradona, like the elite runners who hail from Africa, serves as a model for what can be achieved on the world stage, provided you have the requisite temerity. And though the money hasn't reached anywhere near the heights of professional soccer players, winning a major marathon can go a long way in transforming the local economy of a dispossessed or oppressed people. Running is the Kenyan variant of American hoop dreams, just as playing in a premier European league is the gold standard by which footballers play the beautiful game.

Maradona's legacy, however, is not simply that he played in Europe, but that he made it look easy, inevitable, the well-deserved spoils of being a genius on the pitch. When Eddie Van Halen, Maradona, or Kipchoge are in the thick of the shred—when they are in the moment of doing what they were born to do—they smile with a childlike joy that transcends the furrowed brow of concentrating adulthood. They have entered into a world somewhere beyond the trappings of the everyday grind of capitalism at work. And we, in turn, are transfixed.

We may have
forgotten along
the way that this
dynamic otherworld
exists, that it is
actually within
our reach as well,
that genius begins
with the everyday
dream of a better life,

that in risking vulnerability—the proverbial "putting oneself out there"—lies the possibility of the most radical, transformative kind of joy and purpose. And whereas world records are made to be recorded, then broken, this kind of radical transformation remains a fount of possibility within us, waiting to be called into action.

While I was trying to cough up a few miles in Fargo this weekend, Catalonian ultramarathon maestro Kilian Jornet Burgada (KJB) was attempting to break the world record distance for running twenty-four hours straight, held since 1997 by the great Greek Yiannis Kouros. KJB's attempt was done around a track in Norway, one lap at time, with only a handful of other participants to break up the monotony. Unbeknownst to me at the time, KJB had already quit when I checked in online some thirteen-plus hours into the race. He apparently dropped out around eleven hours and 134 kilometers in, then spent the rest of the night in a hospital. At least they have a national healthcare system in Norway, am I right? All kidding aside, this is part of the risk that entices someone like KJB, who is still one of the greatest who ever lived, someone who ended up having an off day running his first ever time trial on the track.

Born in 1956, Kouros is rather a contemporary of Maradona's, as deserving of membership in the athletic pantheon as anyone. His record for twenty-four hours is 303 km, or 188 miles—or 7.2 marathons back-to-back at a 7:37 pace. Which is absolutely insane. In addition, he has run the next *ten* longest distances for twenty-four hours. He claims his mind tells his body it's not in pain, and his body believes it. I don't know how tall he is.

I check the computer clock, and it says 2:42 p.m., which would be a marathon PR for me. Is it still within me? I wonder. In the zone, in the moment: a mutual sense of purpose and belonging comes when we feel this inner within-ness. Within-ness is when I go from playing with words to feeling like I'm inside a poem in the making. When I go from jamming a new chord progression on the unplugged Telecaster to rocking out with the band. When I go from grumbling about the cold and generally feeling off to simply shredding the miles. If you catch me inside one of these moments, you might even see the sincerest smile flit across my face.

Around 30K into the 2013 Twin Cities Marathon, I started believing I wasn't going to bonk. I just needed to stay relaxed, cross the bridge into St. Paul, and not overthink the long, steady incline up Summit Avenue. Then a spectator off to my left shouted "great smile!" to me, something no family photographer or Grandma Trussell could ever coax out of this sullen kid turned cynical adult. Was it that obvious? One can only hope the flush of the marathon-in-progress hid my subsequent blushing at being called out. Smile? Wasn't me, I swear!

Then again, nothing prevents me from reading this as a moment of collective ecstasy, written into the cosmic fabric of the sport itself, as true as Eddie Van Halen still needing a band, Maradona a team, and Kipchoge a training squad in Eldoret. Joy and greatness must be reciprocally shared, experienced together, or else it doesn't count.

December 2, 2020

Lonna told me yesterday that she had seen *two* woodpeckers pecking at the house, not just the one I'm daily shooing away from the back wall of the sunroom. They are persistent buggers, to be sure, and now I fear a couple of them is looking to nest *chez nous* for the rest of the winter. I plugged a quarter-sized hole with steel wool a week or two ago, and now they're pecking below it. I can't help but think that these territorial fuckers have chosen their spot, by hook or by crook. They can't help themselves, I know, and while I admire their instinctive audacity—also knowing that ours is one of the few houses with wood siding left in the area—I was hoping the oncoming winter would keep the birds from perpetrating too much buckshot damage on this half of a former farmhouse built in 1908.

You have to seek out the little perks of the winter season, like having a few months respite from loud student parties which periodically result in vandalism and damage. Once someone smashed Lonna's rear windshield with a half-empty bottle of Smirnoff Ice; another time some miscreants dumped an entire recycling bin of plastic bottles on the front lawn. I could go on. Now they are building five-story dormitories across the street from me, essentially so a couple of students can pay twice my mortgage to live in a two-room apartment adjacent to campus.

Some other critter or family of critters is making a burrowing ruckus under the porch as well, right where the hornet infestation a couple summers ago took place, where the groundhog lived for a time in the late aughts. I've never wanted to live in a fortress. Even when Samuel Traut was murdered across the street in the summer of 2015, I didn't invest in a home security system. I haven't fixed the lock on the garage, either, nor did I repair the chain-link fence on the side of the house that some reveler bent out of shape one night. I let the invasive vines and anthills take over the lawn, and I cheer for the rabbits of the neighborhood. They say that the cockroaches are meant to outlive us, which means that at some point we'll have to put in with the cockroaches.

Way before the pandemic—in fact, since moving here in 2003—I've felt rather cut off from neighbors and neighborhood, and that is on me as much as it is on them. I've gotten to know the cool students almost exclusively through Beyond Running. I only attend North Dakota State University's campus events infrequently, the built-in excuse being that I teach across the river, and so am more likely to feel compelled to attend one of Minnesota State University Moorhead's myriad events. That said, I get the feeling that very few people on either campus—any campus?—have the time or desire to attend non-sporting events. Most clubs seem permanently fledgling, most readings and lectures sparsely attended, and now, with enrollment taking the next plunge in a decade-long nosedive, once-irreplaceable curricula seem to have lost their place as well. Long before the pandemic came to campus, the halls of academe turned into a living mausoleum, largely devoid of the hustle and bustle traditionally associated with higher education.

Though administration typically expresses its gratitude this time of year, and generally tries to put a happy face on the gutting, it's hard not to get the visceral feeling that all of it is going away. I fear I'm even getting used to seeing my academic life flash before my eyes. I'm considering which courses I'd like to teach one more time before I'm compelled or coerced to move on from my life's career path. It probably doesn't help matters that I just started reading Kim Stanley Robinson's *The Ministry for the Future*, the near-future dystopia, which we are witnessing with every fire, hurricane, and act of international profligacy.

So where is my happy place, my smile at mile nineteen? How far do I need to go back in time to find a photo of me without that thousand-yard stare? Even photos of me at three years old seem to have it—unless Dad caught me unawares—the look of a tentative kid with some vague presentiment that all this, too, shall pass. My dissertation from the previous millennium concerns not feeling at home in one's home, but of course you don't finish and defend something having figured it out. I just proved what I asserted last time: twenty-five years is next to nothing.

I've trained myself to keep hold of more renegade smiles from previous shreds. Lonna snapped a pic of me smiling at the end of the Dick Beardsley Half, the month before Twin Cities Marathon 2013, which was my FB profile photo for a few years. And my brother-in-law Chris Bick took a pic of me with a mile-wide smile at mile eight of Boston 2014, which then made its way around the internet well before I made it to the finish line. And of course, the Jackson Day Race 2019 finish, of which there is sadly no photographic record.

Though I know that it's hard for me to pull off a fake smile, the more I integrate the smile of deep contentment and awakened concentration into the shred, the better off I am. Relax the jaw, keep the arms loose, turn on the furnace. There is a season, churn churn churn. Keep looking up, keep looking ahead, keep looking around our home planet. What do you see?

December 3, 2020

Four miles at 6:47 pace yesterday, completely gray out but relatively little wind for once. I was celebrating reaching 40,000 words, another arbitrary milestone that lets me know I've still got some skin in the writing game. This morning I put on Robyn Hitchcock and did my strength workout first thing, intoning my sometimes mantra "active electronics" as I try to activate all muscle groups, arms and legs and feet and torso and neck (including the nape, or nuchal alignment) and jaw.

After a mere
fifteen minutes
or so I am
firing on all
cylinders, and
can read
my body
like a book.

I look at my right foot's bunion, the result of cutting the foot open in the '70s, which required four stitches at the time. Coincidentally, and perhaps predictably, it was one of Dad's many metal bookshelves in the basement that sliced my foot open, while I was playing hide and seek. I can't see the scar on my back from Dr. Dean's treadmill in 1982 or 1983, when I slipped and my shirt got caught in the belt I'd been running on a second before, but I know it's there.

I've got a very visible scar above my right eye that's almost twenty years old from falling over a bike rack drunk in the Twin Cities after a Guided by Voices show at First Avenue. What you're seeing when you look me in the eye are the trace of my glasses, which split open my forehead while my skull audibly smacked the pavement. Not my proudest moment, to be sure, but in the interest of full disclosure, I confess it here. There is a reference to the scar in the song I wrote "Capture the Flag": "from the light of neighbors' backyards, find your home / the scar is just a poem left alone" (even the elemental possibility of neighbors made it into the song!). If I look at my right pointer finger, I can still see the mark—more like a pale striation, actually—from my first pocketknife, another holdover from the '70s, around the same time a firecracker blew up in my left hand. I was no doubt trying to throw it at someone, just another day in the life on Harvard Street in Arlington Heights.

I never broke any bones, at least not until I cracked my sacrum on August 27, 2014. And though I've never run over seventy miles in a week, I was clearly overtraining and over-racing. I ran four marathons in thirteen months—Rome, Grandma's, Twin Cities, and Boston—at least ten half marathons, and numerous five- and ten-kilometer shreds. I started believing I was impervious to such wear and tear, that I was going to keep increasing mileage and intensity until eighty-five miles a week was no big deal, just part of the training.

And so, after a month or so on crutches and several months off the shred, I started running again, only to crack my sacrum in more or less the same place, just on the other side. After having to bail on a fall marathon, I was trying to get in shape for Boston 2015, but ultimately had to sit that one out as well. I went to Boston anyway as both qualifier and spectator, and watched Chris and Tanya Hass from Beyond Running—as well as then-president of Minnesota State University Moorhead, Anne Blackhurst—take the right turn onto Hereford and head for Boylston Street and the finish line. No matter what, I get chills just thinking about this part of the course.

Not surprisingly, I'm not the only one sifting through the tea leaves of the early '80s to see what's left of my misspent youth. The resurgence of interest in running is but one connective tissue in the aging body of American life. Everything is being remade; '80s music and film isn't so much revisited as it is reimagined or repackaged. I'm currently working through the *Cobra Kai* series, the so-far brilliant contemporary reboot of the *Karate Kid* movies. Though there are indeed elements of camp and cleverness to the first five or so episodes—references to Bananarama pancakes and Ratt ringtones—it is beyond smart in its depiction of Daniel Larusso and Johnny Lawrence as adults, as well as high school and Los Angeles in the 21st century.

In order to confidently navigate the horrors of high school, I needed something more than being second "man" on the varsity cross-country team. So I spent a good chunk of freshman and sophomore year at Mike Zimmerman's dojo in Mundelein, Illinois, in the hopes of gaining the confidence and ability to defend myself from the taller, larger, and generally meaner jocks and burnouts, most of whom had little to no appreciation for running as a sport. I went into high school believing that—as a shy weakling barely over 100 pounds—I wouldn't earn respect from my peers so much as become a target.

Though I didn't exactly progress in martial arts—I called it quits after one tournament, and never took any belt tests—karate changed the way I felt about my body and my abilities. I became way more flexible to start with and learned to do pushups on my knuckles and fingertips. Though I took to *katas*—the solo forms whose imagined fight sequences look somewhat like interpretive dance—I was cagey about sparring, and always seemed to get the wind knocked out of me. As with running, yoga, and meditation, karate is all about breathing; you focus on the breath, which you come back to again and again, breath being that invisible force which stokes the furnace and activates the electronics.

I still know the seven hand strikes—although I got briefly hung up on the sixth just now, the palm to the nose—as well as the three major defensive blocks. I have deep-seated memories of that time, from running a few miles with Sensei once to having to spar with him. As he casually landed strike after strike, all the while cajoling me to fight back, I was trying to wrap my head around this most absurd predicament I'd found myself in. Did I really sign up for this?

After what seemed like forever and without really thinking about it, I managed to land a left ridge hand on Sensei's neck. I figured that Sensei would make me pay for it, and so I immediately started apologizing. Sensei said, "No, that was *good.* You have a fast ridge hand." And though I've thankfully never had to use one in a real fight, I know the ridge hand is still in my arsenal. Like so much of that year, the ridge hand is a vital and elusive part of the elemental story of my education-age body.

The Karate Kid came out in the Orwellian year of 1984, the same year as *This is Spinal Tap*, and the year before *Rocky IV* and *The Breakfast Club*. This means I must have started karate before it came out, and it wouldn't surprise me if I'd all but given up on pursuing the martial arts by the time I saw the movie in the theater. By the end of 1984, I had run my last cross-country or track race. And though John Hughes's classic was filmed on the North Shore of Lake Michigan in Illinois right around the time I stopped competing in the area, I didn't identify in the slightest with any of the kids depicted in *The Breakfast Club.*

I may have traded in my *gi* and running spikes for a guitar and turntable that year, but the song remains the same. At the twenty-year high school reunion—which itself seems like a long time ago now—classmates still asked me the perennial question: "Still running?"

December 7, 2020

Another Monday in the land of the plague. One in ten North Dakotans have contracted the coronavirus, although the real numbers are undoubtedly much higher, as we are ritually and regularly reminded every weekday morning by Amy Goodman on *Democracy Now!* Some days more people are reported to have died of coronavirus in America than those who died in the Twin Towers attacks on 9/11. Some days more Americans die due to "complications" related to COVID-19 than the total number of Japanese fatalities since the pandemic began.

I'm not big on any holidays, to be honest, but as a lifelong academic I tend to appreciate the holiday season, the wax and wane of each semester punctuated by regular breaks in the week-to-week activity on campus. Even during this pandemic sabbatical, I have anxiety dreams about not being prepared to teach, not being able to find my classroom, running late to the all-important first class of the semester. Even a sabbatical feels like a vestige of or throwback to a former system of education that valued the idea of a semester or year of recuperation and refocusing—as well as the university's erstwhile investment in the idea of intellectual engagement writ large. This year has come with the realization that my life's work is coming to an end, that the very nature and value of literary study is shifting dramatically, slouching towards extinction. It is all going away, and you are reading the words of a dying breed.

We celebrate this month with Peanuts and the Vince Guaraldi Trio on heavy rotation, albeit in a rather non-denominational fashion. Vince Guaraldi, who died of a heart attack at age forty-seven. This morning, I put on a morning raga from Ravi Shankar before switching to Laraaji, still a go-to three months into this sunroom quarantine reflection. December is turning out to be weirdly autumnal here, with lots of sun and temps above freezing. My colleague and comrade Travis Dolence told me last night that it even hit the 50s yesterday.

Instead of running this weekend, I did some random chores, like putting a coat of linseed oil on the garden boxes we bought from J. Earl Miller way back in May. Though we weren't very successful in growing vegetables and herbs this year, it felt good to support J. Earl, who has had to be creative in finding ways to pay the bills since March. I thought I might plant some garlic in them for next year—I read in the newspaper you could do that—but like most things, I let it slide. With all the time in the world, I barely managed to find an hour to keep the red cedar boxes from turning gray.

Once I get going, though, cleaning feels good, and I end up washing throw rugs and recycling cardboard boxes, then sifting through the shifting piles of papers until I gouge my head on the island cupboard like an idiot. Then I have to watch as many Premier League soccer matches as possible, icepack pressed on skull, while thinking about running without actually doing any.

The shred goes on without me. In Valencia yesterday, running history was made: four men went under 58 minutes for the half marathon, breaking Geoffrey Kamworor's record of 58:01 from last year in Copenhagen. The winner in Valencia, a city already home to 5K and 10K world records this year, was Kibiwott Kandie, who ran an absolutely insane time of 57:32. That's around 4:23 per mile for over thirteen miles (or twenty-one kilometers). I'm wondering if I could run 400 *meters* at this pace. Maybe, but what about 2:12 for 800 meters? Doubtful. Nevertheless, like a commanding Chelsea win against Leeds, it sure is beautiful to witness.

And now I find myself on the verge of crossing another imaginary finish line, that of 42,195 words, one word for each meter of a marathon. Though I know it's a another completely arbitrary milestone to reach in terms of writing, so is the marathon distance itself arbitrary, as it is reputed to have been adjusted to suit the desires of Her Royal Highness for the 1908 London Olympics—the same year someone got the bright idea to build this house, as it happens. The 1896 Olympic Marathon was around forty kilometers, or twenty-five miles. So, I guess we have the British monarchy to thank for the global—pantheistic?—mystical identification with the most hallowed of running distances. If for some reason you think the actual distance is ultimately no big deal, try running 26 or 26.1 miles and calling it good. The fact that more and more often a marathon comes down to the wire—not altogether very different from a 400-meter event sometimes—only adds to the mystique.

Whether running or writing, in-person events have been largely canceled or made virtual until at least the summer—and then who knows? Though there may be some global optimism regarding potential vaccines making the rounds these days, the numbers domestically are less than encouraging. I see the word "raging" at the end of encouraging, and it seems a fitting descriptor of the contemporary American zeitgeist. I could use a 42.195-minute evening group run with the Beyond Running crew to remind myself how rage naturally succumbs to the power of shred. Every singular time.

Some stadia in England are letting in a couple thousand fans, which in Chelsea's Stamford Bridge isn't even one-twentieth of its capacity of 41,837. Come to think of it, it would be super cool if the Bridge had 42,195 seats. That said, two thousand fans in a giant stadium, be it Wembley in North London or Anfield in Liverpool, make all the difference in the world—just as two spectators cheering on a random corner of a local 5K make a difference. To call this kind of spectating "bearing witness" may sound pretentious to some, but I miss it more than I care to admit.

And so now we are nearing the end of another arbitrary milestone of time, that unwieldy entity called the year. As Jay Griffiths illustrates in *A Sideways Look at Time*, a fair amount of human fiddling with natural, elemental, recursive time goes into making 365 days of roughly twenty-four hours apiece count as a global marker of linear progression. I think about how many times we've wished for 2020 to finally end, even as we disavow the awful truth that the end of the year doesn't really mean squat. 2020 may stick around for a while, an unwelcome squatter in the timeshare referred to as 2021.

I think about how many generations, migrations, and translations have gone into any contemporary believer's sacred text, as well as the hallowed nature of the passage of time. Employing this rather outdated idiomatic expression infers an intimate correlation between time and text, going so far as to suggest that time itself is the most sacred and singular of narratives. And like a poem, it has traveled the world for untold eons before arriving at you, here, now.

Who are we when we're not afraid? Why do the most singular and momentous occasions hinge upon eons of time travel? Who do I become when I stop running scared, and start running sacred (cue X lead singer Exene Cervenka's second solo album)? If I just switch some of the letters of some of the words around, might I find heretofore unheard-of anagrams for freedom, justice, belonging? I won't be long. I want to belong. Has being been in the longing all along?

I think it has. To do, with belief. And so, I run with it.

Beatlemania

She remembers your name.
She forgets the word for help.

She remembers to dismember
her glasses. She cries because

she has no eyes. She returns
after a word from our monsters.

She laughs when she's unsleep-
ing. She knows the idea behind

squirrel, but not said word
for. She sings she said I know

what it's like to be dead.
She forgets John is dead,

how the walrus was Paul.
You remind her over and

over. You remind her of
someone she used to love.

Now you are a so-so Yoko
to her Beatles. She won't

want the impromptu omelet
to ever end. She loses herself

in an ether/or mirror. You
hold her hand while you sing

I want to hold your hand. You
drive her car while you sing

Baby, you can drive my car.
She forgets about the moon.

She forgets your name. She
echoes love you with you.

She remembers George is
dead. She can name Angie

in two notes. She knows
your eyes are watering.

She regrets the word for
calendar. Her shattered

glasses reflect semblances
of bird. Forget he said she

said. Forget the idea of
entelechy. She radiates with

the primordial fitness of
planets. Entrusted to her

care are little fidget units
of memory blip. Know that

a warren of hapless rabbits
is still a warren. Or consider

a rafter of turkeys decamping
within her ever after. Forget

about mocha, forget about
straw. Be her moon, be in awe.

December 9, 2020

A mere two and a half months after running my first marathon at age twelve, John Lennon was murdered in New York City. Yesterday marked the 40th anniversary of the tragedy. I remember those late '70s, early '80s days, the Iran Hostage Crisis, the second British Invasion of punk rock morphing into new wave and hardcore, Carter conceding to Reagan, John Hinckley Jr. and Jodie Foster—and, as always, the eerie prospect of high school looming on the horizon. Sometime around then I read *The Catcher in the Rye*, the book Mark David Chapman had on hand when he shot Lennon. It feels like forever ago, it feels like yesterday. Paul, I do and I don't believe in yesterday.

Though many years would be ticked off before I would hear tell of psychologist Timothy Leary and the psychedelic mantra of "turn on, tune in, drop out," I still have brief flashbacks of the '70s on the regular: a girl in third grade Catholic school announcing that her parents were voting for Carter, glimpsing a clip of the Sex Pistols playing "God Save the Queen" on TV, my soon-to-be stepbrother beating a kid with a metal volleyball pole in Runaway Bay, a window in Deer Grove with a black-and-white photocopy of Mickey Mouse giving the finger to Iran, my stepdad thundering down the road like an angered bison, playing solo imaginary baseball games with a tennis ball against a fieldhouse wall, wandering around the Galena Territory with my best friend Mark, the kid who convinced me to read *Watership Down* one year. If I stare into space long enough, I start to piece together a sort of childhood.

If twenty-five years is next to nothing, then how about forty years? At the tail end of 2020, 1980 is coming back to haunt me, I suspect not for the last time. Coincidences seem to run rampant across my memory, crossword clues meant to solve the puzzle of my life: hotel where Lennon was shot or current place of residence? The Dakota. On the radio back in the day, John Lennon posthumously sang nobody told me there'd be days like these, which makes Lennon himself a tragic truth-teller, the shadow of Odysseus's Nobody returning again and again to the scene of the crime to warn us about our future selves.

You can run out of ideas, or run out of steam, but you can't outrun your shadow—or your past.

You can misplace your past, however. You can forget the time when music, running, and reading were your salvation. I've switched to second person only because I'm looking at a self-portrait in a convex mirror (see Parmigianino [c. 1524], Ashbery [1975]). It must have been a decade or so ago that Mom gave me and my brother each a personal box of memorabilia from those days. Mine had various ribbons, photos, and news clippings—once I was interviewed by the local newspaper about running—basically, remnants from my past life as the geekiest middle-schooler around. I seemed to have lost the box in transit, although for the life of me I'm not sure how this is possible.

The box must have also contained my copies of the iconic Jim Fixx running logs, the original daily planner for runners and joggers from all walks of life, as well as an annual companion piece to his 1977 bestseller *The Complete Book of Running*. I don't have to close my eyes to see that glossy, bright-red cover with Fixx's legs in mid-stride, or the year the log switched to an equally brash blue background, perhaps to complement the 1980 release of the aptly, albeit unimaginatively, titled follow-up *Jim Fixx's Second Book of Running*.

One year I had a knockoff running log with a puke-yellow background and smaller text on the cover as well. but the Fixx logs came first and have won first place in my heart. Sometimes I even get the crazy notion to bring them back. In the comments below, tell me how much you would pay for an old-school shredding log.

Jim Fixx was instrumental in getting people off the proverbial couch to get outside and try out this whole running thing—or jogging craze, if you prefer. Looking back, it may be hard for some to discriminate Fixx's impact from the larger health and fitness trends of the era. Jane Fonda's signature workout book came out in 1981, as did Olivia Newton John's smash hit "Physical." Even at the tender age of thirteen, I knew she wasn't talking about exercise, but the video on MTV—Music Television was born on August 1, 1981—redirected the suggestive nature of the tune.

But whereas these two examples serve as quintessential '80s flashbacks, Jim Fixx is decidedly '70s. You can't evince the Peloton or Strava future with Fixx the way you can with Fonda, who may end up being remembered more for the workout book than the movie career.

Just as with *Kramer vs. Kramer* (1979) post-divorce, I remember Mom and me watching the 1980 film *Ordinary People*, Robert Redford's directorial debut set in the suburbs of Chicago where I grew up, in the theater together. We must have both been looking for meaningful clues in Hollywood's magic mirror in those days. Unlike the madcap cast of characters populating the more popular John Hughes catalog, I identified with Timothy Hutton's suicidal character before it would occur to me to ideate about suicide. Every movie—like

> every movement—
> comes with
> a cast of shadows.
> The movie may
> not hold up,
> but the world
> it is refracting
> is lurking in
> the penumbra
> of their memory.

A former smoker who wrestled with weight issues—unlike Bill Rodgers, incidentally, who was just a former smoker before winning the 1975 Boston Marathon for the first time—Fixx wasn't writing to me or my demographic, but he forever changed the way I moved through the world. I still recall the pithy anecdotes and advice punctuating those running logs, the lined paragraphs of each week of the year urging me to go out for a run, and then write about it.

Jim Fixx died of a heart attack while out on a run in 1984. Not only did the autopsy reveal that he had three seriously occluded arteries at the time, he was also genetically predisposed to suffer heart trauma. Putting aside the crossword-puzzle coincidence that 1984 is also the year I saw the band The Fixx on the *Phantoms* tour at the Aragon Ballroom in Chicago, trolling Wikipedia for vestiges of my past running life reveals a rather startling, albeit coincidental, factoid about me and Jim Fixx. His birthday is April 23—attention Shakespeare scholars—and he died on July 20, which means he died at age fifty-two and just shy of three months, or the same age as I am today.

The more I sift through the shadows of my past, the more suspicious and superstitious I become. Did this really happen the way I think it did? Am I taking too many liberties with my troubled past? Why do I start out thinking about John Lennon and end up googling Jim Fixx? Perhaps I'm stripping coincidence down to its original core, its temporal "co-incidents," to see where I fit in. I haven't run in going on five days now; what would the phantom of Jim Fixx do?

That answer is obvious, at least. Jim Fixx would do as The Beatles and follow the sun.

December 10, 2020

So, I followed the sun for four miles at a 7:02 pace, thinking of the Talking Heads song "Once in a Lifetime" and the early MTV days again: same as it ever was, same as it ever was. After name-checking the *Phantoms* LP and giving Gracie some affection on the new Casper bed, I laced up a pair of Ghosts and embraced the eerie "every day is Halloween" pandemic holiday season. True to form, the government is busy employing old-school methods to screw over the American people: namely, passing into law a stimulus package with no stimulus checks. The 908-billion-dollar package is roughly half of what was on offer the month before the election and is clearly and woefully inadequate in addressing the fiscal and human carnage wrought by the American response to combatting the virus.

Meanwhile, the talking heads on CNN and Nancy Pelosi have the audacity—of hope?—to suggest that the American people do not really need a stimulus check right now. I'm not joking, or even ranting, although I should be. Yesterday, I watched the head economic analyst on CNN, Matt Egan, say that most Americans would probably just save any check they received from the government. That seems to go for the tens of millions of people facing eviction, the tens of millions of people without employment or health care, and really everyone who received the first stimulus check over eight months ago. It must take a special kind of hutzpah to be such a willing servant of the US propaganda machine—and, of course, regular stimulus checks deposited in one's personal bank account. Ever notice how our leaders and analysts routinely assume that all Americans have stock portfolios, own property, go to college, or have such things as bank accounts? Hindsight is blind-sided in 2020.

We interrupt this rumination on running and being to assess nothing less than the death of America's soul—an assertion three days ago by the former MSNBC talking head Krystal Ball. We can look to the example of at least a couple dozen nations for ways to take better care of the American people in a time of pandemic: namely, paying anywhere from 75% (Canada) to 100% (Japan) of its people's salaries. Unemployment stays low, businesses stay in business, everybody wins. A humane response to the crisis is not rocket science. Indeed, it should be the easiest, most natural thing in the world.

The only thing our elected representatives have in short supply is empathy. Perhaps it has been bailed out of them. Perhaps empathy—and lack of empathy—follow the logic of trickledown economic theory, but I suspect the working class and small businesses alike are used to making do with no love from up above, and so must generate empathy on their own. We have learned to internalize that help is not forthcoming, that the accountants will not be held accountable, the leaders won't lead us to safety, the Labor Secretary will be anti-labor, the Defense Secretary is really an Offense Secretary, and so on—irony as ideology. I look at the vast and vastly ungeneralizable sociopolitical landscape of America and see how we are united by a virulent sense of deep-seated futility, an infectious apathy, anomie, and antipathy towards the world at large. I can't say I blame us.

North Dakotans are getting a somewhat earned national bad rap on this front, with the persistent questioning of mask mandates and such being at the forefront of the diatribe. I say "somewhat" earned, because it's all too common to excoriate and demonize the behavior of one state or population, or one half of the country, to absolve oneself of any wrongdoing.

I personally have spent the year trying not to let rage or antipathy be my default setting when I go outside, or get behind the wheel of a car, or see someone not complying with basic quarantine guidelines. Myriad times throughout any given day in Fargo can seem like a kind of free-for-all, when all I really want for America in 2020 is liberty and justice for all.

Many of us can hearken back to the flood of 2009 as a kind of pre-emptive counter-narrative to many contemporary kneejerk media-driven polarizations: Minnesota v. North Dakota, rural v. urban, white folk v. everyone else, etc. As an eighteen-years-and-counting resident of Fargo, North Dakota, who works across the river in Moorhead, Minnesota, I have found this first psychic polarization to be the easiest to undo; most days it happens as a matter of course, whether that course consists of day-to-day errands, the Fargo Marathon or the Red River floodplain.

So, when schools were canceled and millions of sandbags needed to be filled and stacked throughout the Fargo–Moorhead area, we filled the campuses and sports arenas on both sides of the river to do what needed to be done to save each other's homes. I suppose it's so much easier to come together when you can literally come together and literally share the load—as well as have the sense that, though not in sight, the end must certainly be just around the corner or bend in the river.

We in Fargo–Moorhead have never needed extra encouragement to socialize—even if it involves the rather arduous task of damming (and damning) a flooding river—and such a motley gathering would seem particularly natural and appealing to the runners in the area. After all, racing is about getting up extra early to get to the course on time, and then getting everyone else who shows up across the finish line. You may hope for good conditions, but you know not to expect them. Ultimately, we are running to feed this vague and almost-forgotten hunger for community and belonging, to joyfully and purposefully move in holy communion towards the soul of ourselves that has gone missing. We give us this day our daily shred.

It doesn't take very long to forget what communing feels like, not weeks or months. It only takes a couple of days not running for my body and mind to start conspiring to keep me indoors. The non-runner in me takes over, the thought of exercise feels more like a chore than a gift, and I stop desiring the unmediated company of other human beings.

Even after a lifetime reaping the benefits of running, I'm trying to find a reason to tack on another rest day. This trending toward inactivity in isolation ironically unites me with the world at large, as we mutually forget how we used to use body and mind to feed each other's souls. And this fact of daily forgetting in America, in turn, explains what running can offer the citizen hampered by the pervasive sense of futility coupled with a lack of empathy: regular, joyful communion; common purpose; peace in heart, body, and mind. For starters.

On a lighter note: my go-to beer this week is a pilsner crafted by the Fargo Brewing Company called Stimulus Czech. The can even has an image of the signature $1200 check—in case anyone has forgotten what it looked like, I figure. As the suits in DC haggle smoke-and-mirrors-style over how to sell the American People a stimulus package without any stimulus checks, I find Fargo Brewing Company to be more than ruefully clever, more than nudge-nudge wink-wink regarding the current state of affairs. While I drink my Stimulus Czech this week, I will think further on how we can save local businesses like Fargo Brewing Company. And I will look forward to resuming Tuesday-night beer runs at FBC when it's safe to do so.

December 16, 2020

RIP Harold Budd, American ambient composer, eighty-four. RIP John Le Carré, British novelist, eighty-nine. RIP Marvin Bell, American poet, eighty-three. RIP all victims of COVID-19, the American tally of which has topped 300,000. I'm in the ironic sunroom on day whatever in the year of pandemic, feeling slightly guilty for enjoying the morning coffee while listening to Tommy Guerrero's *No Man's Land* on YouTube. I have a feeling I won't run today, that I'll watch two Premier League matches on Peacock whilst drinking my Stimulus Czech in a Junkyard stein and wait for news of my comrade Andy, who was admitted to the ICU in Chicago on Sunday night with diabetic—diabolic—ketoacidosis. Andy, who I'd implored to take care of himself just last Friday during our weekly Zoom meeting. He'd been feeling poorly for a couple of weeks, has pre-existing health conditions, as well as a job as a labor organizer for the Illinois Federation of Teachers clearly running him ragged.

Andy spoke of how the obligations of his job were largely self-imposed, but also that he didn't want to let his many constituents down, who are constantly under threat from above. Tom reminded him of the purloined letter truth-bomb that if he doesn't take care of himself, he won't be able to take care of anyone else.

We hold
these truth-
bombs to
be self-
evident, but
all-too-
often find it
impossible
to change
course mid-
life sentence.

I joined AARP recently, which apparently means I have signed up for monthly reminders of my age group. Though fifty-two years young, there is, of course, no turning back the clock. I read the interview with Bruce Springsteen about his new album while recalling seeing him with Mom and Ryan Jerving—my grade and high school friend who taught me how to play the guitar—in 1984 at the beginning of the *Born in the USA* tour. I'm already writing about John Lennon and Jim Fixx when the AARP magazine shows up with testimony regarding John's untimely death at age forty.

I think about the age of Lennon and the Age of Lennon at the same time, Lennon's death as the crease of an eighty-year novel we've had to complete without him. Kafka died at age forty as well, in 1924, just shy of forty-one. I'm coming to the end of an epic novel for which there is no sequel. There is so much left to write about, so much to run towards. I was just thinking of the word "trammeled." Now there's a word with some weight and heft, usually used in the negative. Both words were lying dormant in my mind, and now they're stretching their legs, preparing to travel the untrammeled path towards my elemental and ecstatic being.

When my father turned seventy, he said he still felt like a kid—this despite inhabiting a body that caused him severe discomfort until the end of his days. I believed Dad at the time and didn't necessarily want him to grow up and face the music that his ailing body was failing him, compromising the avid child inside. I knew he could eat better. He could have stood to walk around the block at least once every day of the 21st century.

I, too, often feel younger than my years, but two summers ago I felt like I'd turned a half-century three months early. The child in me screamed I was too young for this shit—which I suppose I still prefer to feeling the opposite. Curiously, AARP preys on both sentiments at the same time: too young to really identify with the senior demographic, too old not to cough up the modest fee for a five-year membership. We all know I'm not getting any younger.

Do we have any say in determining when we slow down? When will the seven-minute miles become unimaginably fast for me? What is the relationship between talent and desire? Why are we so good at disavowing the unhealthy costs of a particular regimen, job situation, or lifelong habit? The answer to this last question must have something to do with how we as Americans are acculturated, how we learn to naturally intuit that a department of Health & Human Services exists to make it harder to get healthcare, how addictive food is by nature unhealthy, how most diets are just another commodified form of addiction, how The Who's "meet the new boss same as the old boss" worldview expresses a very American sense of futility regarding one's gainful employment. We most certainly will get fooled again.

Despite our acculturated talent at disavowal, we all know that the planet is dying, that healthcare should not be tied to employment, that beneath the surface of skin we're not all that different from one another in the end, that we could learn something invaluable from how we respond to our pets every day. How we want to make every day count, because ten to twenty years is nothing at the end of the day.

I don't want to bum anybody out, but the initial distribution of the vaccine happens to come with the possibility of the next virus—a new strain of COVID-19, perhaps to be called Covid-21?—as my London-based YouTube soccer mates chatted about yesterday. Meanwhile, my man Andy is admitted to a Chicago hospital ICU with a blood sugar count over 600 (80–120 is normal). His neighbor in the hospital was suffering from a gunshot wound, and a screaming COVID-19 patient apparently kept him up all night as well. What's more, they are running out of names for hurricanes.

As for the more mundane question of my running body letting me down, I can be more optimistic. A patina of new snow on the ground, I ran five gray and windy miles at a 7:34 pace three days ago—which means I got out there despite the weather, not that I'm slowing down. Though I wonder if I can still get in shredding shape enough to PR in my 50s, I'm confident that I can keep dialing in the sevens for a good while yet. I've always maintained—no pun intended or avoided—that it's a kick to win a race at my age, but on this fraught and auspicious morning I wonder if it's more than that. To finish strong is to kick-start the epic and uncertain future.

December 17, 2020

I blame the person from the Faster. Stronger. Runner. conversation stream who recently liked my one-word Facebook comment from a lifetime of ten weeks ago: "tempting." It was October 1, and I was referring to registering for Grandma's Marathon 2021. While offering a virtual option as well, the in-person full and half marathons are capped at 4,000 registrants each. The ever-popular Garry Bjorklund Half had filled by October 2—no surprise there—and this morning a mere 251 places remained for the 26.2-mile event. A few clicks and some credit card information later, and I have all winter and spring to get serious about the training. My Beyond Running friends are already in shape, as is my poet-marathoner comrade Fred Schmalz in Chicago, apparently, so that leaves me to contemplate and commit to more than a few short shreds here and there—and only if the temps and the wind don't dissuade me from putting in the miles. I now have six months to prove I'm made of heavier mettle.

Even with the vaccine, there is a decent chance of cancelation, as even the Fargo Marathon's typical May running has been prudently postponed to September 25. Come fall, there could be a whole host of major marathons getting their sea legs back, as it were. Along with the August Olympics in Tokyo, we could see Boston (September?), Berlin (September 26), London (October 3), Chicago (October 10), *and* Tokyo (October 17), as well as Twin Cities, et al., run within a mere few weeks of one another. When you consider such a hopeful glut of marathon possibilities, my registering for one of the few summer marathons available sounds relatively prudent: fewer participants, for one thing. Surely, the major races aren't going to be able to have 50,000 runners next fall. Duluth isn't exactly an urban center, and the course itself skirts Lake Superior, starting twenty-five miles out of town in the unassuming North Shore hamlet of Two Harbors.

The last time I ran Grandma's Marathon, in 2016, it was sweltering hot, and I ended up tacking on over a half hour to my 2013 time of 2:49:30. In 2013, I was a decidedly naïve marathoner at the tender age of forty-four, having completed Rome three months earlier in 3:03 and change, as well as suffering from some serious hypothermia for a couple hours afterward in a medical tent outside the Coliseum. At Grandma's 2013, Fred ran a tick over 2:40 that year, after dropping me at mile eighteen, and I remember being ridiculously disappointed at having broken 2:50 for the first time ever. Now I look back and think how incredible it was that I held it together relatively well in the second half, even after Fred was long gone. The second half of 2016 took me over two hours to complete; in 2013, it took me around eighty-eight minutes. Three cheers for naïveté.

I can't remember the last time I let my guard down or the last time I truly relaxed. My jaw is an underpaid prison guard with a sharp stick up its ass for yours truly. I don't feel like I'm having conversations as much as I'm watching myself try to act normal while aping the normal conversational conventions. I once told Lonna—so many years ago—that I only feel whole when running. I'm not sure if that's quite true, but I appreciate the sentiment. An idea that's been knocking around in my head for some time now: running can offer completeness, but not completion. In life, we are recursively circling around our soul—the one Krystal Ball suggested that we have lost last week during her "radar" on The Hill—and running provides a singular access to our elemental and elementary being.

Like Boston, Grandma's Marathon is a point-to-point course, and the shuttle bus rides to the starting lines of each race seem interminably long. And yet, the first half of a marathon always goes by quickly, no matter the course. Even when far from being in shredding shape, I usually just soak up the first half, and it's typically over before I know it. I don't look at a watch or overthink the race ahead. Sometimes I know I'm fit to bonk by mile eleven (Boston 2019), or the halfway point (Twin Cities 2019), or mile fourteen (Rome 2013). Other times the bonk comes a few miles later, and twice in my life it never truly showed up (Twin Cities 2013, Chicago 2018).

In addition to my PR performance at Twin Cities 2013, Grandma's 2013, and Boston 2014—my third- and second-fastest times for the distance, respectively—are the only marathons where I kept it together enough to get under 2:50. You see, I had remained naïve enough in my old age to believe that getting under three hours—the time that had so obsessed me as a twelve-year-old—would be a given, even on the worst of days. Little did I know that things could go even worse—much worse, in fact—than that hypothermic 3:03 in Rome that kicked off my reboot as a marathoner.

Since Grandma's 2016, I've been fond of saying that whatever particular marathon I just completed would be my last. All the months of training and yearning and visualizing just for another conspicuous notch in the bonk tree: it's so not worth it! Sometimes, especially when I'm muttering the marathon's last rites not so quietly to myself on course—someone always hears—I believe my days as a marathoner to be over.

And then I'm thrown an incredible and undeserved bone, like a 2:55:38 on six weeks training at age fifty—mark it, Dude!—and I think I must be overthinking the marathon, that it really is a very elemental distance that shall reside eternally within me, whether run in the Eternal City or in Duluth, Minnesota, in the age of pandemic. The spirit of the marathon lives within, an everlasting pilot light in the holy furnace of shred. See also the two moving documentaries titled *Spirit of the Marathon*, the first filmed in Chicago (released in 2007), the other in Rome (2013). Seems like it's time to complete the trilogy, wouldn't you say?

So, overthinking the marathon? Guilty. But over thinking the marathon? Decidedly not. For now, any training will serve as a Get Out of Jaw Free card. For the time being, I have a shred date with destiny in a good six months.

December 22, 2020

We're set to get above freezing today, probably for the last time this year, and maybe for the last time until April. You never really know, although Fargo has already been anticipating the bitter, bitter cold for months in body and mind. You know it's coming; you hope it's not as bad as last year.

Coming up on seven years ago next month, I joined the YMCA on a day that was well under twenty below zero. I'd rarely been on a treadmill since scarring my upper back on one thirty years earlier, and I hoped that in the ensuing quarter-century treadmill technology had advanced in terms of both functionality and safety. That said, I've always maintained that my fall in the early '80s was due to a combination of ground control and pilot error.

I was running at the founder of the Liberty Road & Track Club's (LRTC) home, a medical doctor who'd caught the running bug the first wave around. The LRTC was at heart comprised of avid neophytes mesmerized by this bulky contraption in the den of Dr. Dean's home. I slipped on the human conveyor belt as we ramped it up to a four-minute mile pace. Four minutes flat, I should stress. It would be another year before I'd throw down a 4:57 mile in gym class sophomore year, and though I'd broken thirty-five minutes for 10K a couple times in my early teens, going so fast the first time on a new toy was supremely foolhardy. I didn't think to avail myself of the guardrails or the stop button, wasn't clipped in or anything—and to be honest, I can't visualize any of these features when I flash back to that fateful evening. There's just the tread, and the speed, and the spill.

Now I'm flashing back to the first time I mounted a horse, courtesy of Mr. Ralston, some Marlboro Man-like friend of Dad's who had a ranch in Volo, Illinois. I must have been about eight years old. As soon as I got up there, the horse started bucking uncontrollably, and I started bawling immediately. My first horse ride could have been measured in seconds, appreciably shorter than anyone's first attempt at rodeo. It would be some thirty years before I'd risk getting on a horse again, this time at the tail end of 2003 on a family vacation in Costa Rica. I got through it, but I didn't enjoy it.

For the record,
you're not going
to get me to

zipline or bungee
jump or try out
any of that so-
called extreme
shit. But I hope
my fondness for
horses affords
me better inter-
actions with them
in the future.

Around this time, I was also attacked by a duck at what I must have misinterpreted to be some kind of petting zoo somewhere in Illinois. But that's another tale of woe for another time. Just remember: do not pet the ducks.

Of course, everyone in LRTC saw me slip, then writhe on the treadmill while screaming "turn it off!" over and over until they did, several seconds or hours later. And of course, Dr. Dean's daughter Shannon was having a slumber party that night, so she and her friends were also witness to my losing battle with the impromptu mediaeval torture mechanism that perhaps all treadmills remain at heart. I seriously doubt any of them took up running after that particular slumber party, at any rate.

I can't blame the treadmill for my shyness, my categorical inability to talk to girls, or my polymorphous fear of the unknown. But at least there was a doctor in the house. In the following weeks, Dr. Dean would end up cleaning the third-degree burn on my back at the hospital more vigorously than Mom could bring herself to, given my tendency to wince and moan in mortal agony when she did.

I'd already missed the eighth-grade Wendella boat trip in Chicago. A reward for being a member of the National Junior Honor Society in good standing, I was set to soak up the Highland chapter of NJHS's only perceivable perquisite, that being a field trip to the Windy City, where I'd gone to the top of the Sears Tower for my 7th birthday—this despite my trenchant fear of heights—and where I'd run a number of races with the LRTC before starting high school cross country in the fall of 1982.

I may have already run my first marathon in under three and a half hours by eighth grade, but I was having serious trouble getting the hang of putting things in my eyes—namely, contacts, which at the time came in "hard lens" form to correct astigmatism. You had to build up to wearing hard lenses all day, so my goal was to show up with lenses in, and then pop them out on the boat. You know, casual and whatnot. Instead, I ended up getting a lens stuck in my left eye, and subsequently had to go to the ER to get it extracted. I'd somehow embedded it in the corner of my cornea, and as I recall, it was none other than Dr. Dean who was on duty that morning, and who dutifully got the lens out.

Apparently, I'd managed to scratch my cornea with all that ocular fiddling. Even with all the advances in contact lenses over the years, I've never considered trying them again; nor have I been even remotely curious about Lasik surgery. I have a phobia about my eyes being popped or scooped out by some malevolent force, and I find eye drops quite unpleasant, almost impossible to administer. So, forty years later, I get a new pair of old-school spectacles every few years and am considering "eyeglasses model" as a late-stage career possibility. Like books, glasses will never go away, not completely—and I shall use both in tandem every day for the rest of my life.

My general moratorium on treadmills, however, had to be lifted in early 2013 to accommodate an inexplicable desire to shred. I still don't know why 2012–13 turned out to be different than the previous twenty-five to thirty years of hibernation. I'd spent the previous decade gauging how much worse winters in Fargo were than elsewhere in the Midwest, how one learns to intuit the difference between five above and five below—as well as five below and fifteen below—the way I learned to interpret the chasm between 100°F and 108°F in Phoenix-Tempe, Arizona. I might quip on occasion that it's a dry cold in Fargo, but only in the knowledge that we also get the "wet cold" variety: thirties and humid, windy, bone-chilling cold, Norway in November.

To survive winter running in Fargo, I attempted to adopt some general rules, such as the base temperature has to be double digits above zero if I'm going to venture outside. That means it could "feel like" 20 below, but I need the temp to be at least 10°F—and preferably 15°F—for me to shred outside. I could bend this rule if running with other runners who don't make rules other than the one about a treadmill being an absolute last resort. Now, uncomfortable with using a public treadmill in a pandemic, I'm going to have to come up with some new rules.

Meanwhile, we've booked our non-refundable accommodations for Grandma's Marathon in June, which means that we're set to spend a long weekend in Duluth, race or no race. Mom will be there, and hopefully, Hass will take me up on my offer to run it together. Hopefully this will mean more than the first half of the marathon, as turned out to be the case with Twin Cities last year. Dave Sapp from the Beyond crew is signed up for the half as well, so marathon gods willing, June will augur a collective return to shred.

In Dave's garage on Sunday, I watched the hundred-person Marathon Project in Chandler, Arizona, in which seven American men ran under 2:10, and Sara Hall came in under a minute off Deena Kastor's American record for the distance. Though I didn't run during my nine months in the Phoenix area—I preferred to hike around South Mountain before heading to the Rio Salado brewery, which was hidden in an industrial park south of Guadalupe, or to TT's Roadhouse in Mesa—my Pavlovian marathon mind started drooling at the prospect of 45°F and next to no wind at the start. Next to no wind is a dream come true for me.

Though I didn't make it to the group eight-mile run beforehand, something about watching a race with four other running geeks reminded me—I might even go so far as to say re-bodied me—that shred is a dish best served to a team.

We rattle off random stats while taking in and assessing all the micro-moves of a marathon, biding our time, not getting ahead of ourselves, until the end comes and I'm on my feet screaming at the leader, Martin Hehir, to quit looking back at Noah Droody and get after breaking the 2:09 barrier. With a little over 200 meters to go, Hehir does just that, breaking the tape at 2:08:59.

Sometimes I surprise myself by how much I care about someone like the undeniably elite, but relatively unheralded, Hehir bringing it home during a pandemic marathon "project," but then I realize that the inexplicably overinvested spectator is a role I naturally fall into, anytime and anywhere we decide to block off car traffic to run as one. I will shout myself hoarse on your behalf if I think it'll get you looking forward, grinding out the next stretch, and owning the finish line as we all run for our lives.

Purr

for Gracie

Sonic equivalent of fur. The body traps
its dud bomb and disperses the tender
udder thunder. A chair and a tree are
the same thing. A table has leaves, and
people also leave. Every thing leaves me
questioning: what wall art, which font?
No, tiny lion, I'm even unknowing about
in. In is of itself, uneven. I'm only sure
of purr. I only think in numbers between
one and one. Hurry is just one more thing
other animals do. O my, we are a genuine
broken record. We, perpetually deterred
by the indeterminate half-life of purr.
Take me, for example, not for one second
worried about the many steps in between
our little giggle of minutes, not even
stopping to look at the dog-earing animal
magnets or trying to get my bearings. I'm
only leafing through the lifelong photo
album to get to there's you, there's me.

December 24, 2020

I'm going to have to come up with some new rules if I'm going to train seriously this winter. This morning my cellphone informs me that it's currently -8°F but feels like -28°F: the kind of bitter cold Steinbeck references in *Travels with Charley*, the Jack London winter blue-face special that would be incomprehensible to my fair-weather friend Adam Hodges in Houston, where these days it might drop into the 40s at night.

I spent the night before last listening to the 50-mph winds pummel the screens in Hero's room—Hero being our erstwhile hyper-vocal, snow-white cat who we put down not two months after Dad passed in 2018. For the record, I was visiting Mom in Michigan at the time. Now Gracie has claimed the room from her late sister, as well as the entire upstairs floor. Once the epitome of feline poise and dignified taciturnity, Gracie now howls every morning: for water from the bathroom shower tap, to be lavished with affection on the futon in the orange room, to have a few treats in between treks, and then to recycle the trifecta of drip-pet-snack until long after Lonna and I have gotten out of bed to attend to her every whim, and maybe, just maybe, move along with our day.

That's what you do when it's true love; as fellow teacher and cat lover Michael quipped back in the spring, there are sure going to be a lot of depressed cats when this is all over. When I first took up the professorship at Minnesota State University Moorhead in 2003, I was so anxious about getting a good night's sleep that I tried not to pet my cat Harold when he joined me in bed in the orange room, Harold who at the merest touch of a human hand would purr like a snowmobile (or lawnmower, if you prefer a warmer image). Harold passed in 2005, but I still long for a sleepless, purr-filled night with that charcoal-gray charmer to while away the midnight hours in the redeye of the pandemic.

I'm talking about cats, but I'm also talking about pacing, and the search for what's truly meaningful in the ultramarathon of life. Pacing means being in the moment, a moment which is never static, but rather ecstatic, ex-static, set into motion, involving an intent and concerted unfolding of, or opening up to, the momentous. Tensile (but not tense) and wiry (but not wired). The sinewy slow-twitch muscle of shred nurturing its singular and overwhelming fast-twitch shadow. Always imminent, always immanent. Brimming.

Metaphorically speaking, we are running into the shadow of the future. When you literally run with and towards your own shadow, you enact a model of the passing of time. The goal is not to catch one's shadow, which is obviously impossible, but to let it pace you moving forward. And when you run with the sun at your back, you begin to play shadow, to glisten, to listen, to enlist stillness to be at the behest of ecstasy. A moving tribute. Elemental education. A statement of purpose.

I'm momentarily hung up on that phrase "moving forward," which has inauspiciously entered our vernacular, along with other default chestnuts like "unprecedented" and "thanks for reaching out." In the end, however, it's not very hard to return "moving forward" to its literal and elemental meaning. Some languages use one word to signify both story and history (histoire, Geschichte, storia, etc.), and in some Romance languages "tempo" (or temps, tiempo, etc.) signifies both time and weather. What if Proust was also in search of lost weather? What if we made a practice of returning to the elemental nature of original meaning? We face the music of the future with the past on the tip of our tongue. Singular and plural. I and You. Reciprocal echoes intoning Kate Bush's "Running Up That Hill": if I only could, I'd make a deal with God, and I'd get him to swap our places. This existential songline runs throughout *Hounds of Love*, all the way to the album's final track "The Morning Fog": I'll kiss the ground . . . I'll tell my loved one[s] . . . how much I love them.

Here's another elemental expression that needs to be returned to its original hammer-throw brilliance: ______ is so basic. Breathing is so basic, clean drinking water is a basic human right, and so on. I love building up base mileage but hate doing junk miles. Every mile or kilometer—every meter, every step forward—is part of basic training, a basic element in the periodic table of shred. So, after years and years of periodic practice, what's my next move? The answer is elemental.

As I reach the finish line of another year—a year with no in-person races, serious training, or regular mile/weather markers, for that matter—it feels like everything is left to be done. This is potentially a good thing; the practice of getting back to basics is a prelude to shred. In 2020, I never got up to speed with training, I bonked midway through life's journey, I ran out of time and weather. I moved forward at a snail's pace while the pandemic sprinted ahead, which can only mean that

from now on,
every corner
or cave of
future meaning
shall come
with the caveat
of a mean
new normal
going viral.

And as the temp of the day slowly moves onward and upward at snail's pace—almost noon, and the phone now reads five below feels like 25 below—I have a lot to be thankful for. Namely, a functioning furnace (knock on wood), which has served me well both literally and metaphorically since I switched it on in September. I don't mind that it may have taken an ultramarathon-length reflection of more than 50,000 words and counting to rediscover the elemental long-distance relationship between running and writing, moving and being, creating and surviving: it was in the longing all along.

The next move is to take the sporadic base-mileage training to the next level, to incorporate different workouts every week to sharpen and strengthen the forward-looking movement of shred. It means embodying and envisioning a running-being practice that, even in the smallest and seemingly most inconsequential instances, reaches out to the world writ large. The shred is my holy writ. Just as the original meaning of "threshed" is to stamp with one's feet, shredding is threshing meaning, stamping the very earth with our earthly approval. I don't have to be running to set this world writ large into motion, either, but I do have to have faith in the idea of moving toward a better world. Movement longs for a movement. Teams meeting, mates teeming.

Signing up for a marathon that may or may not go off in six months signifies a relatively short-term but significant commitment to training, to teaching body and mind to learn to be in loving lockstep with one another come June. But I already know that I've set the stakes significantly higher for myself. I'm writing with body in mind and mind in body, thinking about the elemental cadence of every poetic foot, every unprecedented narrative movement.

Rule number one of marathon training is to get to the starting line healthy, which means the movie of my next six months shall be called *A Prelude to Shred*. It is an epic tale at the tail end of the ouroboros of time, the search for humanity in the postscript of the humanities, the not-so-quick-and-easy errata of a quixotic knight-errant who travels at the elemental speed of shred, the ecstatic pace of peace.

SHRED!

mutually assured

. . . and if i make of my body a planet . . . and if my lungs are crematoria . . . and if my brain is the parent company of a pesticide giant . . . and if my skin is a fraying map of conquest . . . and if my epiglottis is a terrorist cell . . . and if every cell is a cellphone . . . and if my tongue o my tongue is an incarcerated torture victim . . . and if my breath is a vanishing ozone layer . . . and if my ribcage is a warzone . . . and my heart an improvised explosive device . . . and if my clavicle is a dump truck heading to the refugee camp in my throat . . . and if my pelvis is a jungle earmarked for slash and burn . . . and if my ears are life rafts for orphan children . . . and if my glands are a global pandemic . . . and if my capillaries are an invasive species . . . and if my eyes are mercenaries . . . and my intestines a landfill . . . and if the rape of my genitals is a fact of daily life . . . and if my blood is oil . . . and if my language is on the endangered species list . . . and if my dandruff signifies nuclear winter . . . and if my cheeks bear the weight of a dying sun . . . and if every follicle is a passenger pigeon . . . and if every pockmark is a mirage in the desert of my back . . . and if my nostrils implement the latest fracking technologies . . . and if my soul o my soul is doing time for identity theft . . . and if my teeth are Stonehenge, the Berlin Wall, and the Rosetta Stone all in one . . . and if my hands are mercurial dictators . . . and my nails bullets . . . and my fingers guns . . . and if every hiccup launches a drone strike . . . and if my appendix is an offshore account . . . and if my nervous system is the internet . . . and all my neurons profit margins . . . and if my pulse is a mass protest . . . and my jaw a mass grave . . . and every word a gravedigger . . . and if my dreams are cryptocurrency . . . and if my late-stage dementia presents as late-stage capitalism . . . and if my elbows and knees arm for Armageddon . . . and if my arms drop the mother of all bombs . . . and if my forehead is in lockdown . . . and if my solar plexus is a new doomsday machine . . . and my bones an ice floe for the last polar bear . . . and my legs the last forest preserve . . . and if my eyelashes are a lynching mob . . . and if my scars are cave paintings . . . and if my spine o my spine is the Great Barrier Reef . . . and my bellybutton an hourglass . . . and my neck a museum of natural history . . . and if my temples have become tourist visitor centers . . . and if you, my interplanetary dust mote double, should decide to come visit me . . .

January 6, 2021

Same as it ever was? Surely, a new year by design portends—or at least encourages us to consider—turning over a new leaf. Though someone skeptical about just about anything that purports to be new and improved, I'll allow that a new year is, at least in part, what you choose to make of it. To paraphrase early R.E.M., I don't want to go back to Rockville and waste another year. I want to make it count somehow. I want to struggle for social and environmental justice, to run toward a greater humanity with purpose and belief. In 2020, these abstractions—justice, humanity, purpose, belief—were hard to come by.

Meet the new year, same as the old year? Over 350,000 dead and counting in America, and the oligarchs in DC seem to be their typically rapacious, oblivious selves. While Congress was allegedly debating the merits of giving the American people a $2,000 stimulus check, they had no problem passing the National Defense Authorization Act (NDAA) budget of $741 billion. More Democrats than Republicans voted for it, as it happens, and everyone on both sides of the aisle promised to override the promised presidential veto. Meanwhile, the new strain of the virus cares not about the body politic that passed the ironically named CARES Act nine months ago, also known as the largest upward transfer of wealth in human history.

When Biden claimed that "nothing would fundamentally change," he was telling the banks, the CEOs, and the military-industrial complex that he had their backs. Even a pandemic wouldn't make him support Medicare for All; even the myriad horrific recorded incidents of police violence wouldn't make him reevaluate the 1994 crime bill he architected; even genocide wouldn't make him rethink his erstwhile vociferous support for the Iraq War—or Venezuela, for that matter. Apparently, some 30 billion dollars of the NDAA is earmarked to overthrow Venezuela.

We can't even distribute a vaccine or provide clean water to our own people, but something tells me we'll have better luck bombing innocent civilians overseas. To paraphrase Barack Obama dropping a three for the cameras in Michigan in 2020, that's what we do! I read this week that the United States has well over 750 active military bases worldwide. That is what we do. By contrast, China—no champion of human rights, am I right?—has but one foreign military base. It's in Djibouti.

This rueful sense of hopelessness is where I found myself at the tail end of 2020. I think I ran three times in the last two weeks of the year. It seems that every time I try to write myself into a shredding state of mind, something gets upended. It's more than my flow, my drive, my desire to push through the difficult miles of the race that gets compromised. My belief in a better world is shaken to its core, the chorus of Jawbox's "Mirrorful" on repeat in my head: I don't believe!

In addition to running, I look to soccer and tennis for ways to decipher the psychology of belief, to witness how athletes succeed or fail against seemingly insurmountable odds. Players are often called upon to grind out a result or win ugly, and the unbelievable comeback takes its rightful place as the most epic and hallowed of narratives. At heart, we love a good plot twist—as long as it involves our team winning, to be sure—if only because it's more often the case that our teams and athletes seem to be perennially floundering.

The head case trying to find confidence, the team in a slump searching for a definitive victory, the injured marathoner trying to get back into shredding form—the whole desire to flip the proverbial script fascinates me. And when the narrative does change, it almost looks inevitable on the surface, as if the protagonist in the drama has achieved nothing less than changing the course of history, and that she knew she had it in her all along. What is it that Eliud Kipchoge said about running under two hours for a marathon? Anything is possible. Also note that it was his second attempt at breaking the two-hour barrier.

My beloved Chelsea is going through a signature rough patch on the pitch these days. Like my running slump, this is perennial with the Blues. Only a month or so ago we were building the team, starting to gel, looking at a run for the title—and now we're playing like bloody Arsenal was playing a month ago, with no quality or drive. You can see the lackluster attitude of the team in real time, an utter lack of belief in their ability to run the opposing side ragged, often coupled with being a couple goals down by the halftime whistle. Meanwhile, a German club like Bayern München will be two-nil down to Mainz at the half and end up winning the match 5–2. You don't doubt for a second that it's going to happen.

Similarly, the greatest tennis players in the world are never sure—can perhaps never allow themselves to be sure—they're going to beat Rafael Nadal. He's just so annoyingly unrelenting that breaking the master from Mallorca—even taking the opening set from him—is no cause for celebration. Quite the opposite, in fact. If it takes around seven marathons (i.e., matches) in two weeks to win a Grand Slam like Roland Garros, Nadal often seems like he's still training until at least the semifinals. You end up hoping for him to drop a set just to make the match slightly more interesting.

Believing in a different outcome than the anticipated or predicted one is absolutely critical to changing the narrative, and the upset must stand as one of the most elementally moving narrative possibilities out there. They said it couldn't be done, and they were wrong! When you witness an individual athlete or team fight against all odds and expectations—when you see them believe in themselves despite everything occurring around them—you become privy to a transformative psychic moment in which the end result—yea, even a loss—matters less than the mad belief that you or your side will prevail.

So, at the starting line of 2021, I promise Kipchoge that I will run in the belief that anything is possible. And though I know too well how easy it is to stray from the path of justice, how subtly and surely I slip into fear mode as defense mechanism, how my capacity for belief threatens to grow nebulous and distant in the middle of winter, most especially in the pandemic era, I move forward in the knowledge that I've been in these psychological trenches before, and that running offers a singular way out of the epic standoff or stalemate. We're not moving in circles, though the course may be a looped one. We are returning again and again to our mental and elemental reasons for being. We cannot build a proper defense out of fear.

I, for one, need others to remind me what belief looks and feels like. Yesterday, a journalist from Louisiana, Barry Lemoine, sent me the link to an episode of *Go Coast* about St. Bernard Parish and Arabi, which lie a few miles east of New Orleans proper and where the Jackson Day Race is run. I'm actually heralded in the video as the "North Dakota native" who won the race to boot, which sounds more than a little weird to these ears, despite living one-third and counting of my life in Fargo–Moorhead. As I recall, the end of 2018 was rather the proverbial shit show in terms of belief, and I went into the race feeling like I shouldn't even be there. United Airlines had lost my luggage en route to Houston for one thing, so I had to buy all new gear for the race. The few few-mile runs leading up to the race were perfunctory at best, and in addition I was some pitiful combination of drunk and hungover walking to the start after celebrating my labor organizer and grad school friend Andy's birthday with the team the night before—two years ago to the day.

It is not hyperbole to say I came into 2019, a mere two years ago, in the throes of existential despair. I certainly didn't believe in the possibility of change, that it would do what it's elementally supposed to do, which is of course to make a difference. I turned out to be more than wrong, and I'd almost forgotten how wrong until Barry sent me the video link. I still cringe at the sound of my voice, to be sure, the low register of which seems to both frighten babies and put students to sleep. But the elation on my face is undeniable. As if I'd scored a hat trick in the second half two-nil down, as if I'd beaten Nadal, yes . . . Carollo, who dat?

But really, just being with other lovers of shred would do me just fine right about now, any point-to-point or looped or out-and-back course where anything is possible. Fool me once, brutal new year, shame on you. This year, any lack of belief in dynamic transformation is shame on me.

January 8, 2021

While I was writing a couple of days ago, Trump supporters stormed the White House, and started taking the most bizarre, postmodern kinds of selfies: with Capitol police, some of whom appear to have opened the rather laughable barrier—especially given the comparative level of violent clampdown across the country in the wake of George Floyd's murder—between them and the mob; standing on a statue of Gerald Ford adorned with a Make America Great Again hat; sitting with feet up at Nancy Pelosi's desk in her trashed office; in some kind of Dionysian pioneer regalia—everyone's favorite protest garb—as well as the requisite Confederate flags coming out of retirement for the insurrection. I'm sure Don Delillo, author of *White Noise,* flashed back on his life's work and felt some strange cocktail of prescience and obsolescence. America: you can't make this shit up.

If I'm not careful, I'll fritter away the entire morning with the remote, perhaps sucking on both thumbs lest I join the social media fray ruminating in its own inimitable way on the failed experiment that is this great country of ours. It feels like we are witnessing something more than a pandemic of misinformation and corporate greed—though make no mistake, the powers that be are profiting bigly off the current unrest—but rather the birth of a strange new era of global illegitimacy for the US. The birth of an un-nation, a nation in name only, the scary laughingstock of the world. In addition, yesterday's national coronavirus death toll for a twenty-four-hour period approached 4,000, another world record. Do your fuzzy math, America; what is your remainder?

If I'm not careful, I'll follow this omnipresent gray day down the rabbit hole of humanity—not expecting to find anything, mind you, for this hole is undoubtedly bottomless—moving at the speed of virulent desperation, and unfocused, careless rage.

My best on
any given day
is that of
an agnostic
praying to
the elusive
rabbit gods
of shred.

Every day is any given day, to be sure, and this tautological expression reminds me that I've been gifted another twenty-four-hour allotment to give more of myself to the struggle for meaning and justice. In these pages, I've spilled a fair amount of proverbial ink exploring the inkling that it all has to do with the language of running, that all dogma, political or religious or cultural or otherwise, shifts—or pivots, to use the contemporary parlance—when you set yourself into motion. In the end, it's all about the beginning. We need to discover a new direction, a new path; we can't turn back, but we can start over, reset ourselves into epic motion.

I've run three to six miles every day of 2021, a full week of the new year through ice and wind and snow, at average paces ranging from 7:06 to 7:58 per mile. It was completely coincidental that my total for the first seven days turned out to be right around 33.3 miles, like an LP's rpm. More revolutions per minute, please! Like Lonna, I've committed to running at least twenty-five miles a week, patiently building up the mind and body's ability to harmoniously shred at the pace of peace. I wonder if I can run 2021 miles this year, which averages to approximately 5.5 miles a day. It's a goal I'm not worried about right now; I merely want to be more consistent and intentional in my running and being on any given day.

In the intricate math equation of life, of course, there is no remainder. I'm building up to eventually leave it all out there on course. And though I've been at this crossroads many times before, today feels different somehow. Maybe because it's David Bowie's birthday today, as well as Elvis Presley's. I remember listening to Bowie on vinyl all day in my dorm room when he turned forty, in 1987, just some piece of teenage wildlife. And I remember listening to Bowie at the Junkyard Brewery with Lonna's mom when he passed five years ago, on January 10, 2016. I couldn't possibly understand at age eighteen what I know to be the visceral truth today, that sixty-nine years isn't much time at all. I was always twenty-two years behind Bowie, but now I'm slowly and inexorably catching up. And after eight-plus years with early onset dementia, Beth is set to turn sixty-nine on March 22 as well. Today is our given day. Under pressure we're breaking; why can't we give love, give love, give love?

Wilma

is from the Philippines and
must speak in many tongues
when she thinks about home.

She must carry an island
in the Philippines inside her
on her way to work in America

and listen to her life story as
told by my dad who can't not
butt in when we start talking

about when Wilma lived in
the Philippines and how her
first husband often came home

drunk and threatened to kill her
with a gun. This is a true story
about Wilma my dad is telling.

I was the one who went to their
wedding in Chicago in the late
nineties and didn't know a thing

about Wilma or the Philippines.
For example, I thought Tagalog
was her native tongue, but it's not.

I knew the Philippines had been
colonized and we had something
to do with that. Other than that,

something about Spain and 1898,
Japan during WWII, and Imelda
Marcos with her scandalous shoes.

I want to ask Wilma's god why
it takes a lifetime to not quite
get to know someone or something.

Other than that, I wonder about
a young woman in the Philippines
pretending to be asleep, and praying.

January 13, 2021

Yesterday I ground out a modest four miles while Everton managed to beat Wolves 2–1 away. I timed my run so I could catch most of the second half—including, as it turned out, defender Michael Keane's winning header—after seeing both sides hit the net in the first. Beforehand, I also caught Sheffield United's first win of the season, the cursed side grinding out a one-nil result at home against Newcastle, who also seem to be flailing of late. I ran four miles at a 7:07 pace while all the area middle and secondary schools were being let out, adding lots of foot and car traffic as I tried to sidestep the slick and snowy parts of the run.

A dozen determined days of consecutive shredding, and the changes in attitude and intent are almost palpable. Strike the qualifier; I can feel the power of accumulating miles in my flesh and blood, my muscle and bones, the way all of us here in my body are working together as a team. Last week, without trying much harder than usual, I managed to run thirty-two miles, even though I'd set my sights on twenty-five miles like Lonna. When you run every day, it all adds up, of course, and the goal for subsequent weeks becomes incrementally easier in the merely having done this week. I return from an overdressed few-mile phlegm-fest with sweat equity, steam rising from the tights and base layer as I stretch on the front porch.

Even if the run turns out to be a complete slog, I end up knowing my commitment to the practice of shred is stronger, and that this moment of mundane elation is the best I'm going feel all day. There are endorphin-level variations between, say, two miles and ten, but at this point anything in between is guaranteed to dynamically move the mind in the right direction.

Even intimately knowing the physical and psychic cumulative effects of running every day, my motivation to get out there wasn't entirely pure or self-sustaining. I went out when I did so I could have a beer while watching the rest of the match. I almost considered taking one out of the fridge and putting it next to my Junkyard stein but figured that would be a bit excessive. This isn't New Orleans, after all, or even a particularly grueling training effort. But there have been many days during this comparatively mild winter where the beer has taken precedence to the shred. And overall, I've been okay with that—until I wasn't. Maybe it was watching too many YouTubers for too long lay down fifteen miles on any given morning—good on you, Kofuzi, Seth, Andy, et al.—that made me realize I was missing out on some epic fun. Maybe I allowed them to guilt-trip me into getting out there. Whatever the reason, I feel like I'm now nurturing a humble and tiny running streak for the second time in my life.

The first streak started on a random day in August a couple months after Dad passed and lasted 260-some days. Like the goal of running 2021 miles in 2021, I'll reflect on it in passing, if you will, but am content to focus on the beer—or the pizza, or the match—from day to day. Some days promising myself all three of these—this shredder's personal recovery trifecta—seems necessary to get me out the door for a couple miles. The sacred and profane desires to commune, celebrate, and explore are intimately connected within the ethos of shred.

Sometimes I might avail myself of adages like "trust the process," or "rinse, recycle, repeat," or simply "simplicity" three times à la Thoreau in *Walden*. These are intriguing expressions in their own right, but let's see what happens if I put them on their heads for a moment: learn to break down the process, and even "trust the breakdown." Or: repeat after me, singularity, singularity, singularity! Make like eureka, and shred. The moment you start playing with words, you start playing with the stock-and-trade idiomatic ideas that serve as the very foundation of human cognition. In wordplay, like a speedplay or fartlek run, comes insight, surface-level meanings giving way to something more dynamic and resonant—or as the Buzzcocks would have it, a different kind of tension. Intense tensionality. As verbs tense their muscles, we flex our able, tensing a different kind of kindness in kind.

I may just be messing around here, but I'm not simply going nowhere with my thoughts, either. As I keep paradoxically returning to the scene of the singular, I relearn how intricate singularity has always been, how shot through with so many parallel-universe instances of consciousness the singular is. Now ask yourself this singular question slowly and repeatedly—slower even than recovery pace—until you see something behind the idiomatic rhetorical appeal: is it just me? I could get behind such a notion.

When I say a notion, I also mean an ocean.

In the opening pages of *Civilization and Its Discontents*, Freud mentions in passing the idea of an "oceanic" feeling, something he claims not to have ever experienced. One could assume that Freud is obliquely referring to and simultaneously dismissing Jung's notion of a collective unconscious. Admittedly, it's been a number of years since I've read Freud; I used to teach him not too long ago, along with Marx (gasp!), Montaigne, Machiavelli, Voltaire, Kafka, Borges . . . I would love to go on. Not too long ago: those were heady times!

Freud is more interested in the psychology of the individual's place as articulated within the framework of the (Western) nuclear family, which makes him significantly less compelling for the 21st century than someone like Jung, whose ideas on shadow consciousness and the collective unconscious and the like have done more than inspire The Police's *Synchronicity* album—the two title tracks of which intimate more than a potential connection between a salaryman and a loch monster.

The oceanic is dismissed by Freud, I believe, because it smacks of organized religion, and therefore its structure of feeling is immediately suspect. Freud is to classical music what Jung is to jazz; his confessed inability to access the oceanic means that he—like the nuclear family, one would think—won't age well. Now more than ever, we need to think in oceanic terms. If you see this ocean as too huge to contemplate, start with any body of fresh water, then make a sea change of consciousness. Start with anybody—say, me—then make a sea change in how we see each other.

I think of the synchronicity of my dad's widow Wilma, who turns sixty-eight today, and Lonna's mom Beth, who turns sixty-nine in March. Both sixty-eight for the next two and a half months, Wilma was born in the Philippines, while Beth was born in North Dakota. Wilma crossed the ocean to make her way in America and eventually meet my dad, while Beth never left the US. Both of them lived in California for a time, I believe, just as I spent my first birthday in Cali with Dad's Sicilian-American parents. Legend has it they told me to cut the cake, and I did so with my hand. Now I wonder: was it my left one? But I digress.

How far can we push synchronicity? How deep is our ocean? Wilma was a teacher in the Philippines and became a caregiver in America. Bethy may have barely scraped her way through high school, but she devoted thirty-eight years of her life to teaching her daycare kids how much love she had to give them, as well as raising two children of her own. Other people jokingly say "mi casa es su casa"; Elizabeth Gregory lived it. Wilma never had kids of her own.

After Beth's marriage fell apart, she never dated again. Many years after Wilma's first husband kept her in fear for her life, she met Dad, who loved her with the signature passionate desperation of a diasporic Sicilian who's never been to Sicily. She's been working through the earthly clutter he left behind in 2018, and I fear she has many years of sifting left to go.

Now both Wilma and Beth are more-or-less alone with their thoughts most of the time, Wilma in the wake of my father, Beth in the wake of Battleship Dementia. They came into this world at the same time, and all the random actions and decisions of the universe it took for me to get to know them make me living proof of an undiscovered and dynamic ocean of meaning thrumming beneath the play of surfaces.

Now for the million-person question: are Wilhemina Bautista Carollo and Elizabeth Renée Gregory merely two random humble people with an ocean of consciousness separating them? Obviously not, as the universe somehow destined them to become cosmic taliswomen for yours truly. How random, and how kind.

January 18, 2021

This morning marks day five of the undifferentiated gray and drear, albeit without the bone-freezing sub-zero temperatures that usually come with it. Conditions are slick and footing unpredictable, punctuated by a wind from the north that feels like elemental overkill. I ran every day again this past week, even averaging under seven minutes a mile for one run, and logging thirty-two miles total. I can feel the uneven terrain of ice and snow accumulating in the muscle memory of my legs, particularly in the hams, quads, and glutes. I tell myself it's all part of the training, that I'm inadvertently testing and taxing the legs I'll need to handle the downhills of that live and wild Boston Marathon in my future, whenever it shall be.

Have I turned a corner in my training or my perception? It's difficult to say, given that so many of the miles I'm logging don't feel easy or comfortable, as I'm forced to alter my gait cycle to suit the lunar-like setting of my surroundings. In my dreams, I can never seem to get proper footing, or figure out how gravity works to propel me from point A to point B. I'm always running late to the first day of the semester, no matter that I'm not teaching this semester. I'm trying to shred the miles of my mind, and invariably end up swimming in air, like trying to slog through quicksand. The more I lean into it, the more that boa constrictor effect restricts me.

I dream of people without masks next to me in line. I dream of being unable to close out all the pop-up windows on my computer, blurry porno a frustrating substitute for true communion. My waking and dreaming lives now seem to meet up in the middle of a pandemic consciousness, a neither-here-nor-there netherworld that makes a mockery of actual human contact. In the middle of the night, I trade the random anxiety dreams with wayward rumination on the short shelf life of all living things. In the middle of the night, I hope to wake up with Gracie or Woodman next to me, as my cats seem to have things all figured out.

In the middle of life's journey, I found myself in a dark mood. I want to be a human super-spreader of some wild and unbridled global awakening, but I can't even make it to the first class of the year in my dreams.

And yet. And yet, I've not been entirely idle or unfocused, as much as the internal and external landscapes of undifferentiated gray matter would like me to believe. I managed to send out three poems last week, the first time in a good while. No big deal, especially considering a number of friends and acquaintances are releasing their next books and wondering how to structure reading tours to promote them. I even came up with a surefire bestseller idea for a series of crime novels set in the UK and Europe. I may even have to move there permanently for research purposes!

I keep ruminating, I keep kneading the literal and figurative pizza dough. I think about my runner friend Adam Pangrac with a broken collarbone, and how he must be going absolutely nuts to not be able to get outside and shred. At least he's just been made partner at his architecture firm—but work, no matter how rewarding, is no substitute for shredding. So, I keep my streak alive thinking about Adam, who would be running at least two to three times what I'm running right now if he could. In the interest of accuracy, I should probably verify that Adam isn't actually attempting to run with a broken collarbone—I wouldn't put it past him. Instead, I run in anticipation of Adam's recovery in due time, when I will hopefully be able to keep up with him on future long runs. If I had a shred of Adam's seemingly innate optimism . . . I would start a movement of movement and call it Shred.

Running every day for a couple weeks makes the strange familiar and entering the uninhabitable a sacred habit. Rainer Maria Rilke famously looked over a mountainous chasm to write some of his *Duino Elegies*, arguably some of the heaviest verse of high European Modernism. I find the flatlands of Fargo currently inspire a similar existential dread. Who would hear me if I cried out among the hotdish orders? All kidding aside, it occurs to me that running means looking over the edge of perception, and shredding means diving into its fray.

Is micro-compassion the opposite of micro-aggression? Can the little insights in passing encourage us to see the big picture in actual size? Who am I when I run, and equally as important, who are you?

Every winter at some point I flash back to my on-campus interview in December 2002, the precarious drive up from Minneapolis, low visibility and ethereal swirling snow, the dinner with my future Department Chair at Sarello's, followed by a restless night in the downtown Radisson, the bitter cold of the parking lot on the last day of finals, and the herd of great, gray elephants hidden in the dirty, gray tundra: did I really want to live in such an inhospitable place? Did I really want to get back into the classroom? What else could I do that would make me happy? Should I hold out for the offer from Bulgaria? Should I go back to Rockville and waste another year?

The thing about questions—and elephants—is that you never really have to answer them, and they will do the remembering for you. An elephant will remember someone they've been separated from for half a century. So who's in charge? Surely not the one who tries to impede the stampede. Now cue the parable about six blind people touching an elephant, each describing something utterly different to one another—which in turn begs the question.

I am not searching for answers out on the run as much as I am begging the elephant to reveal itself in all its unsayable (more Rilke) and inimitable glory.

> I want better
> memory capacity
> for macro-compassion,
> a training regimen
> that every day
> leans into the fray
> of the hallowed
> everyday.

During those twenty-four hours more than eighteen years ago, I met my Sicilian compatriot from Toronto, Tony, erstwhile owner of Sarello's, which closed in 2015. Tony and I are still here. And I also met my future bandmate Adam Quesnell—though I couldn't possibly have known it at the time, of course—who now lives in Los Angeles. Most everything I love, most everything that has kept me sane—from literature to language to music to Sicily to friendship—can be glimpsed through the prism of that brief nerve-wracking visit. There are myriad and beautiful elephants among us.

Today's Monday morning has come and gone in the sarcastically and ruefully named sunroom. They say a new semester or a new dawn or a new age is upon us, but you wouldn't know it by looking outside. Have we at least turned a corner in our coping with the pandemic? It doesn't appear to be the case, but soon I'll look to the news for confirmation. How many new cases today? There must be some way out of here, said the broker to the chief—those stock-and-trade stock and trade characters who always return to the vaccine of the crime.

So, I go out into the open-air grounds of the minimum-security prison on the surface of the moon for my allotted half hour or so of exercise. And though it's gray and windy and cold and slick and sunless and all that, I note that I haven't availed myself of the SAD lamp during this whole gloomy sojourn. I haven't needed to, though of course it wouldn't hurt, because the pilot light of the furnace has stayed lit this whole time, flickering in anticipation of one ungainly half hour a day to ask the better questions. I suit up in the cocoon of my matching bumblebee yellow-and-black tights and jacket. Running into the wind, it often feels like I'm trapped in gray amber. I know I'm mixing insect metaphors here, but safe to say we're in Rilke rather than Kafka territory. Or perhaps today I'm a kind of Kierkegaard with an escape route: here and trembling, the quickness unto breath.

January 20, 2021

After waxing as poetically as possible about running through the gray, and the cumulative effects of running every day—even after a mere couple of weeks—I went out to keep the streak alive. Crossing Broadway, I saw someone in her driveway wanting to back out and waiting to see what I was going to do. I waved for her to back out onto 11th Street, and she waved back. For a brief moment, it felt like we were working together, driver and runner, stranger and stranger, neighbor and neighbor. I believe we were both masked at the time—although it should be mentioned that Fargo's mask mandate expired two days ago—but our mutual recognition surely must have coaxed a smile out of both of us.

Before you think that I'm romanticizing my whereabouts—or making too big a deal out of a passing occurrence—know that my experience of drivers in Fargo is generally one of conflict, a kind of implicit road rage in first gear, ever ready to ramp things up should the opportunity present itself. It may sound harsh, but the average driver in town eschews headlights at dusk either through willful ignorance or negligence, considers speed limits and turn signals optional, deems tailgating a prerogative, and figures anything that gets in his or her way—be it pedestrian, runner, or cyclist—to be in the wrong.

Sure, there are those, generally of an older generation, who pull the *You Betcha!* move of waving on people who are turning to go first, or who stop in the middle of the street to let someone cross. But my informal survey suggests that it is more likely that the person turning left is talking on the phone and completely oblivious to all the cues that competent drivers take in about their surroundings. To be sure, this switched-off behavior may affect you and me both. I think of the woman who starts the car and immediately begins chatting on the phone, as if she is alone in my chiro's parking lot. I think of the dude in the pickup who yesterday turned into the same parking lot—no lights, no turn signal, and not much slowing down to speak of—only to back up rashly and unthinkingly into a parking space and rush inside without a mask, even though Moorhead's mask mandate is still in effect. I'm right there in my orange car, turn signals and headlights at half-mast to light the way, a veritable fiery beacon of communion in this grayest of gray days. But no one sees me, or if they do, they prefer to pretend like they don't.

A couple weeks ago, a young gentleman rather quickly and precipitously backed out of his driveway while I was approaching on foot. I never assume people see me—in general, it is best to shred defensively—but even so, I moved over to the other side of the road, and then the sidewalk, two fingers tapping my head, as if to say, "think about what you're doing, look around you, make sure you're not backing into anyone or anything." I know, my two fingers are overly loquacious, but it's important on the shred to not let our middle fingers do the talking.

Anyway, I wasn't certain the dude had seen me, until a couple of blocks later when he drove up to me, window rolled down, and said something unintelligible, then drove off in a huff. Apparently, my gesture was seen as an admonishment—perhaps it was—and therefore fodder for confrontation.

And perhaps
you can never
tell people
something they
don't want
to hear—

nor can you insinuate it, apparently. And yet I'm doing my level best to acknowledge we're all bottled up in our metal coffins these days, and, with a couple dynamic tweaks to the default setting, this dude and I could be on the same page. In a better world, this stranger half my age would say "race you to the Junkyard," and I would shout out "you're on!" I would probably lose the race, but I would win the war. We all would.

It's important to remind ourselves that, all evidence to the contrary, we are not meant to be drivers first and foremost. Repeat after me: we can't be all we can be behind the wheel of an automobile. I have to hold onto every time a fellow human being sees me and smiles. And the rage I feel welling up inside me every time a fellow human being doesn't see me or heckles me? I have to let it go. I have to move beyond the gut instinct, the default setting that pits me against a vague and spurious enemy behind every metal coffin.

I didn't set out today to talk about the stranger in her driveway a half mile away from where I've lived for going on eighteen years, but what came immediately after: namely, stepping off the curb and rolling my right ankle. My first thought: well, there goes the streak. Maybe thirty or so seconds later, stop the watch. The sprain seemed bad, much worse than the twist I'd suffered a couple months back. Adrenaline pumping, I turned around and hobbled in pain toward home. I was a soccer player on the sidelines of an endlessly dreary pitch, with no physiotherapist to help me get back into the match.

After a couple blocks, I started thinking about the fact that it was Martin Luther King's holiday, and that here in the early days of 2021, we have fallen far short of the mark in terms of social and racial justice. I thought of Ahmaud Arbery, the young Black shredder who was gunned down by a father-son duo on February 23, 2020, in Georgia, and how the running community reacted to the murder of "one of their own" by running 2.23 miles last May in his honor, shortly before the murder of George Floyd in Minneapolis. The title of an online article in *Runner's World* by Faith Briggs at the time: "Don't Run for Ahmaud Arbery Just Once." Peace and justice need to be at the forefront of our epic and transformative movement every day, leading the way. A pacer of peace in the race for social justice.

So much left to do in this life, and time passing just like in the Pink Floyd tune: you run and you run to catch up with the sun, but it's sinking. Most days, we're moving through the devastated world like ghosts in the machine, running toward the idea of a sun that we cannot see. How like the struggle for justice, and how important to keep moving toward the kind of dynamic, intersubjective world we can all live in. As in The Police tune from *Ghost in the Machine* (1981): there has to be an invisible sun, gives it heat to everyone. So, I did what any dedicated runner would do with a freshly sprained ankle. I kept my streak alive, running 2.25 miles with Ahmaud Arbery in my heart. My pace turned out to be 8:38 per mile. I could feel my ankle wincing the whole way, but it wanted to keep the modest streak alive as much as I did.

After a couple rounds of ice, elevation, and CBD lotion, and a visit to the chiropractor the next day, the sun came out like a cat from a closet, strutting around the place as if it'd always been there. You only need to open your eyes and heart and mind to see it. So, I ran another modest 2.25 miles on the precarious, ankle-spraining streets of Fargo, beneath my strange and familiar shredfellow the sun, at the reverential pace of an 8:38 mile, palindrome and palimpsest my elemental metronome. I'll probably do the same workout today, then go the extra mile for peace and justice tomorrow. And the day after that. And on and on, as long as I'm able.

Please, o stranger
so familiar, join my
movement of movement.
We have much
to run on, so much
more to run towards.

January 26, 2021

Another gray morning frozen in the single digits, with a projected high of 5°F and winds up to forty miles per hour. This is the kind of January we expect around these here parts, where even "feels like 10 below" is comparatively mild to the "normal" lows of -25°F not including wind chill. Lately I've felt quite comfortable going out in the 8°F–14°F range, knowing full well that heading into the wind won't exactly be fun or feel invigorating, at least not until I'm back at the ranch with my feet up, perhaps in front of a crackling fireplace courtesy of YouTube.

I've kept my streak alive, despite the occasional twinge on the top of my right foot from last week's twisted ankle. Recovery, recovery, recovery. It means getting serious about elevation and icing, the twenty-minute sessions with the ice pack an ironic sort of reward for slipping on packed ice. I'm also not a fan of this particular roast of coffee I'm drinking, but I'm relishing it nonetheless. I decide to not turn on the TV for YouTube's endless supply of music, instead opting for Papa M on the outmoded iPod in the Bose base console. The device maxed out its tune capacity many moons ago, and so hasn't been updated or added to in at least a decade. And now that computers like this one don't come with a CD docking bay, it's difficult to make playlists, and darn near impossible to burn CDs. When I told IT I wanted to transfer my tunes to this new computer a couple of years or so ago, they gave me what must be a universal IT look, signifying something along the lines of "Suit yourself. But we won't do it for you."

They did give me an adaptor, however, which allows me to charge my antediluvian Garmin watch every week. I make sure the computer is plugged in, then plug in the adaptor, then plug in the charging device for the watch, and then clip the watch into the device. After a few hours, the watch is ready and waiting for me to give it the go-ahead to shred. Occasionally, I'm informed that I didn't eject or close out something properly. Perhaps I'll want to file a report at some point.

By the time you read these words, however, I should be outfitted with the latest technology, and able to synch the watch up to a camera so I can film the great outdoors that I currently experience a half hour at a time. I feel the need to seriously up my tech game this year. I should have a decent microphone as well, and be on the road to learning how to record, edit, and provide content—musical, visual, and live—to the virtual world at large. I've just committed to teaching an online course in the fall, so I should also show up next semester somewhat adept at holding Zoom sessions, as well as sharing and responding to text, data, and the like. Today, I'm swaddled in a cocoon of relative ignorance, watching fully formed butterflies learn on the job and respond daily to the news of the day.

> Today, I've yet
> to subscribe or
> smash the like
> button or ring
> the bell notification.

But, despite my intuitive reservations, I'm warming up to the idea—like a child dipping his toes in the water before diving into a vast and fathomless fishbowl.

The mention of multiple brand names in this old-school blog entry underscores the compromise of becoming an adept and compelling butterfly in the matrix, which involves submitting oneself to a peculiar kind of surveillance technology, whereby a handful of corporate institutions owns the agora—the internet is a marketplace of ideas, after all—and have the power to adjudicate and censor content at will. The invisible hand of the virtual agora. Who could have predicted that the species would become so enthralled with its own profile, as well as its own profiling? Such an uncanny

> narcissus reflected
> in the blurry waters
> of the virtual record.

Despite such reservations—and the many depths of self-absorption to sink to—there is no doubt a lot of fun to be had swimming in these blurry waters. I don't want to be a jellyfish or a school of plankton forever. I enjoy how local runners and running communities have dealt with the pandemic by going global via YouTube, livestreams, and the like. Here, the worldwide importance of running is celebrated joyfully and naturally. I've certainly learned a lot of contemporary lingo regarding running shoe technology—we do love to talk about the latest models, that's for sure—but what is invaluable to me is the idea behind such deceptively casual conversation: a vibrant and diverse community one can belong to, wherever you find yourself on the road of life. Whereas much of online soccer content thrives by pitting people and teams against each other—I've yet to come across reviews of or chat groups about soccer cleats, but I'm sure they exist—livestreams about running seem to remind us that we are mostly competing against ourselves, and we want to share each other's journey toward those personalized goals. Let it be known that I thoroughly enjoy both genres in equal measure, but I click on each for differing reasons.

The virtual world returned to Chandler, Arizona, last weekend for the Hoka 100K challenge, and Jim Walmsley's attempt at the world record for the distance, which stands at 6:09:14, set by Japanese ultramarathoner Nao Kazami in 2018. By the way, that time clocks out to under six minutes per mile for sixty-two miles, which absolutely boggles the mind. Also note that the female record for the distance is the equally unfathomable 6:33:11, by the Japanese woman Tomoe Abe in 2000. In the two decades since, no other woman has broken seven hours for the distance.

Starting on a dragstrip, somewhat akin to Eliud Kipchoge's initial sub two-hour marathon attempt in Monza, Italy, the admittedly uninspiring course near the highway in some typical Phoenix-area wasteland involved nine eleven-kilometer loops, finishing with a straight half-mile stretch to the finish line. The very antithesis of a 100K trail run, one would say, more akin to Kilian Jornet Burgada's attempt at running twenty-four hours on a track. Because of the distance and the course, it was initially unclear to the second-place finisher—Rajpaul Pannu in an amazing 6:28:31—whether he had finished or not. He crossed the finish line, but kept going, calling out to the no-doubt blurry shapes around him, "Am I done?"

This was Walmsley's third attempt at the 100K world record. I watched him drop the sub-sixes like clockwork for over half the race before he gashed his left shoulder on a protruding fence. Blood dripping from the wound, he kept under world-record pace for another twenty-five miles, even picking it up a tick with around 20K to go. But the final 5K did him in. To watch Jim Walmsley urge himself on through the confusion and pain, to witness him run beyond absolute depletion while watching the world record count down in the upper left-hand portion of the TV, the final stretch now seeming impossibly long—and me shouting at my guy to quit looking at his watch—was an overwhelming and elemental experience, one I'll hold inside me for every finish line in the future. Though he missed the world record by a mere twelve seconds, Jim Walmsley set a new standard. At least for me.

And, of course, as T.S. Eliot reminds us in *Four Quartets*, in the end is my beginning. One could even compare Walmsley's looped course with Kazami's point-to-point course in 2018, which I believe offered the additional advantage of a slight tailwind. But ultimately, that is beside the point-to-point. For those of us who tuned in live, we witnessed a moment of greatness that took over six hours to unfold, a singular and ecstatic butterfly trembling in the screen. Am I done? Yes, catapillar. And hardly.

With a long hour left in the race, I texted a group of seven or so runners to remind them of the event. Some of us had watched the Marathon Project in Arizona together five weeks previous. Because of the timing of the 100K challenge, three days ago on January 23, and painfully aware of the virtual zeitgeist of the week, I knew such communication could potentially open the forum up to a Bernie meme. Sure enough, minutes after Jim Walmsley is recorded slumped in a folding chair, the Bernie meme was shared, on his own folding chair, clad in the now iconic and inane mask and mittens of the man.

The meme is the message. I'm not a fan of them at all and am bewildered and disappointed that so many friends seem to think they're clever or funny. Like the Bernie memes in general, this particular one on a dragstrip in Arizona utterly trivializes the lived experience of Jim's accomplishment, as well as our collective witnessing of one of the greatest record attempts of all time. After five years of Bernie Sanders and the progressive movement being delegitimated and downright smeared by Democrats and Republicans alike, it is now safe to have a meme of him trivialize your favorite album cover. More importantly, the memes unthinkingly celebrate the cooptation of Sanders and the movement he so recently used to represent. Healthcare for all? No, but a meme of George Harrison's iconic post-Beatles triple album, now titled *Medicare for All Things Must Pass*. An end to endless regime change wars? No, more troops to Iraq and Syria for starters, perhaps another coup attempt in Venezuela? The Bernie memes are both dilution and distraction, a way to amuse oneself to death in lieu of advocating for a more just and equitable society. I'm waiting for the memes of Bernie sitting be-mittened in the Occupied Territories, perhaps just behind the US Embassy, which the new administration has decided to keep in Jerusalem. Just saying.

So, I enter the virtual world with the ritual twinge of trepidation, the indoor analog to the flinch of recognition I feel when I finally step outside and into the gray cold netherworld of my home planet. I urge myself ever forward, engaged in an epic quest for meaning. I acknowledge that not everyone comes to the internet seeking revelation and transformation, and that the notion of community can take many shapes. Frivolity may be your coping mechanism, and I don't want to take that away from you. But I sit here before you today, primed and ready to mask and mitten up and head outside my comfort zone in search of an epic and collective shred, that singular, harmonic, revelatory, elemental, dynamic endeavor which brings us closer together. At all moments of this race, we must pace each other.

January 27, 2021

I spent a good chunk of the early morning hours in bed ghostwriting a mystery novel set in Oxford, England, in my mind. I have to say it's one of my better ideas for a bestseller—screw baby steps!—and it should be a joy to write. I should stay coy and cautious right now, but I also feel it in my bones: they're going to make a movie of this novel. David Tennant, Idris Elba—the sky's the limit. You heard it here first.

Getting excited, be it about an upcoming race or literary project, means getting ahead of oneself. Make the t-shirts *before* writing the songs for the band. Robert Pollard, the hyper-prolific songwriter and original member of Guided by Voices, relates in the documentary *Watch Me Jumpstart* how he used to make album covers with his now-recognizable collage art, adding band names and song titles and the like to the mix. Eventually, you'll convince yourself to actually jumpstart this pipedream idea; it's always better to be in a band than dream about being in one. Same with shredding. Do as Bob Pollard and GBV do. Always tell yourself: don't stop now.

Because training in the pandemic era—and perhaps any era—involves playing with the art of the pivot, I opted to go about my day in a kind of reverse order. I want to be okay with switching workout times, my daily routine determined by the unpredictable wax and wane of any given day. It's completely okay if I don't hit my original mileage goal for the week—like last week—and should my monthly word count come up short, so be it. It's quite alright to reach the starting line feeling somewhat undertrained, which in the end is way better than overtraining to make up for perceived lost time or ground—or a wonky ankle.

As always, the weather is a driving factor in my daily algorithm: my shredsheet, if you will. My phone informed me that it was -7°F feels like -23°F at 9:00 a.m. Yesterday's base temperature topped out at a few degrees above zero, so I ran when it was somewhere around 4°F feels like -12°F, probably the coldest four miles of the season for yours truly. To be honest, it wasn't really all that bad, the ubiquitous gray weighing on me far more than the frigid air, at least after the first mile into the unforgiving wind. But today, 23 below sounds ruthless enough that I've decided to wait until after Chelsea play their first match with a new manager, the controversial sacking of Chelsea legend Frank Lampard still making its way through the global pitch of the internet.

I finished Kim Stanley Robinson's latest novel *The Ministry for the Future* in bed, attended to Gracie's every feline whim, took a shower, and even shaved, leaving the Prefontaine mustache for god knows what reason. Then I made pizza dough, alongside a couple rounds of pour-over coffee, and sat down to let my mind run wild on this grayish snow-white screen, so like the great outdoors all around me. Before I knew it, noontime was nigh, the dough was prepped, and Chelsea took the field at the Bridge against Wolves. It was raining all day in London—in the parlance of the commentators, it was lashing down—and it was raining all day in Liverpool as well. Though disappointing in some respects, it seemed fitting that Thomas Tuchel's first match as Chelsea manager ended in a nil-nil draw. Same as it ever was. Manchester United was upset at Old Trafford by bottom-of-the-table Sheffield United, and Everton and Leicester left the pitch with a point each at Goodison Park.

I managed to get in five miles at a 7:25 pace, almost exactly the same pace as yesterday, my gait cycle riding the brakes most of the way, given the precarious conditions. It didn't seem any colder than yesterday, perhaps even a tad warmer. A local middle school's marquee even boasted a balmy 13°F, but who really knows? The dough is ready to go, the running streak is alive and kicking, and I'm both warm and chill enough in the ironic sunroom to relish having completed the classic pandemic trifecta of our daily shred: dough slowly rising on the counter, a solid-if-slippery run through the ice and snow, and words working things out on the screen in real time. A triathlon of body and mind, if you will. Today is a day that lay in waiting, a ministry for future revelry and revelation.

Because of getting roped into teaching an online course in the fall, I have to hammer out a syllabus in the next couple of days. But put the bug in my ear, and I'll run with it. So, in addition to my novel novel idea, my brain is now working overtime developing a graduate-level course on "nonfiction writing for the end times." How very meta, don't you think? Though we're a good seven months out, I have to admit that I'm becoming more and more excited for the challenge, and I am grateful that a colleague bothered to ask me if I was interested in teaching online. Being a literature professor for a living can sometimes feel akin to being a dinosaur. You come to feel like your time is always nearly up, that it's too late to not go extinct.

Thinking and writing about—and running toward—the end demands a dynamic momentum, a belief in an end yet to be written. My mom is known to read the last page of any book first—

something I never do—but perhaps I've inherited thinking about endings from her. And then there's the whole question of kismet. The last line of Kim Stanley Robinson's ambitious and often stunning novel, mostly read in bed in the early morning hours: because we never really come to the end.

Lonna and I snatched up two of the remaining twenty-five slots for a mid-May half marathon capped at 300 in Brookings, South Dakota, some five weeks before Grandma's Marathon in Duluth. Though I'm not banking on either race being run, it feels right to at least simulate training for a specific event, one that leads into another, all the while remembering that I'm registered for the Bix 7 in late July and should also keep my eye on the Coloma Glad Peach Run in Michigan, as of now scheduled for the following weekend in August. I also received word that the Boston Marathon will indeed be run in October, and that my time from Chicago 2018 will qualify as a BQ (Boston Qualifier) this year. It's all about the BQ, right?

Will there ever be an end to the pandemic? How will we know when it's over? What about the next, more virulent, more devastating, more untreatable, more harrowing malady? Can we imagine the end of endless war? Can we upend the rates of extinction, the language of despair? In the end is our beginning. Let's get after it!

February 1, 2021

Thirty-one days of running in a row, and now we've arrived at the shortest month of the year. I ended the predominantly gray month of January by running ten miles at 7:23 pace with three other dudes from Beyond Running yesterday, over a light-yet-annoying patina of snow on the ground that made it difficult to get any purchase or push-off. I broke out the slip-on cleats—of which Yaktrax are the Kleenex or the Xerox, i.e., the brand that becomes the name for the thing itself—twice this month; the first time they stayed on and seemed to help, the second time they came off around three or four miles in, and I ended up carrying them the rest of the way. No one tells you that when the wheels come off, you have to carry them with you.

I hadn't planned on running ten miles yesterday, actually, having run seven miles at a 7:15 pace the day before. I figured the group would at least start out around eight minutes per mile, or even slower, and that I could peel off if I just didn't feel like slogging through the run. I'd logged thirty miles last week already, so the ten-mile shred put me at forty miles for the week, the first time in quite a while. I recall having promised myself that I would run ten miles at least once during the month of October in order to demystify that double-digit figure. Though I was some three months late on my promise, long run, consider yourself demystified.

Lonna, to her credit, has run ten miles three times in the last month, and has achieved her goal of logging at least 100 miles for January. Unbeknownst to me until this morning, my friend and colleague Travis ran every day last month as well, racking up some 120 miles for the month, just shy of four miles a day. I write you this morning whilst basking in the gray of the unsponsored sunroom, the new Tommy Guerrero album, *Sunshine Radio*, on the TV, having run some 145 miles during the month of January. My new calendar in the running room so far has no X on it, the classic signifier that means a day that just passed me by, a day I survived without shredding, an unknown quantity of a day that came and went.

Some months go by, and it seems like nothing has been accomplished—or worse, that I'm somehow spinning my wheels in reverse until they fall off. Then, out of nowhere, I have a week where a lot seems to get done, a week in which milestones are surprisingly met apparently through no intention of my own. Last week I reached the late miles in this manuscript; I revised my poetry manuscript *Rabbit Manifesto* for the umpteenth time; I developed that graduate-level course on nonfiction writing for the end times. I felt like a writer, runner, thinker, reader, caregiver, cat lover, and human being all month long, and now I feel ready to shred it forward.

The commitment to regular running enables this general sense of wellbeing. It hones my sense of purpose in the universe and allows me to approach the world outside with the intention of doing right by my fellow animals, human and otherwise. Deceptively mundane tasks like doing laundry or making pizza dough—which we're currently out of, but I can easily rectify that—begin to embody a deeper sense of awareness, and offer more profound insight into the inner workings of my dynamic place in the world.

Despite the fact that I've been having troubled sleep, that Beth is slipping away from us, that Gracie Cakes is aging way too quickly, that I haven't seen my mom in well over a year, that my Press and University—my very livelihood and life's work—seem to be going the way of the dinosaurs, or that I disagree with friends and colleagues on the regular on Facebook—which you should never ever check first thing in the morning—and despite the larger realities of the pandemic, the dying planet, the war machine, etc., I feel imbued with an imminent and intimate sense of potent potential. On this day in 2021, there are more reasons than ever to keep moving through—to paraphrase friend and poet Paula Cisewski—the threatened everything. I hope you'll join me.

February 4, 2021

Around fifteen years ago, my friend Carrie showed me an article about elephants in Africa that has stuck with me. I don't remember if the author was an animal psychologist or cultural anthropologist or what, but the gist of the article is this: there has been a significant increase in unprovoked elephants goring human beings. With alarmingly dwindling populations, in no small part due to poachers ignoring the ban on ivory, the elephants have started to fight back as a last-ditch effort to save themselves. Furthermore, the author opines that their behavior suggests that elephants—one of the most intelligent and empathic of species on the planet—are becoming aware of their own imminent extinction.

This is not a story about a single family or herd of elephants responding to being under siege, but a tale of collective reckoning, a moment in elephant history wherein an endangered species recognizes its number is all-too-soon to be up, that future generations of the species are not a given.

> What presents as
> violent, psychotic
> behavior in some
> elephants is actually
> an expression of
> the most profound
> grief: the end of
> elephants writ large,

the awareness of a mass species extinction from which there is no turning back. The end of elephant days.

Do polar bears have a similar awareness, even though they're often depicted as a species that swims solo towards an ice floe that is always farther and farther away? Is this also why pandas have such trouble procreating, some vague presentiment that bringing a child into such a world is a dicey proposition at best, a procreative act of futility at worst?

These days I often feel like an elephant. I've had too many future-looks-bleak discussions with my literary herd about dramatic and irrevocable program cuts, which in academic parlance is referred to as "sunsetting," or layoffs, which admin refers to as "retrenchments," and whether literary study and the humanities writ large can survive the slash and burn. Whether we're talking ivory tusks or the so-called ivory tower, we're observer-participants of the collective gutting of our kind. The university environment is ritually and routinely deemed unsustainable at these meetings, and we leave with a visceral sense of elephantine awareness: our whole way of life is going away.

These days I also feel like a rabbit, often a literary one in particular: Fiver from *Watership Down*, the prescient visionary of the group, the timid and diminutive Cassandra figure who realizes first that the warren is under siege, the one who feels the urgency of flight most acutely, and also the rabbit least likely to be believed. Those who warn about the end times are usually dismissed casually and categorically—at least at first. A seer initially sees things no one else can see; then these things become what everyone chooses not to see. Disavowal is both a powerful force and psychic survival mechanism. Keep your head down, keep doing the best job you can, things will turn around.

No one wants to be the canary in the coalmine—but the teachers of today are birds of a feather, tasked with looking into the gaping maw of the end times, acutely aware of the precarious and unsustainable future teeming all around us. On a personal level, this starts with looking at teaching particular courses for the last time—as well as courses about the end times—and writing to you as if my very wellbeing depends on it.

Because of course it does. I want to leave something behind when I set out for Watership Down, but I write knowing that there are no guarantees, that even something as esoteric as a local academic legacy is highly unlikely. It may be all Efrafa from here on out.

At one department meeting, I'm warning the warren that everything we hold dear is going away, and my fellow rabbits bristle at my doomsday predictions. We become adept animals at talking around the elephant in the room. At the next meeting, even the die-hard believers in the benevolence of the powers that be start to question the assumption that our Department will exist longer than the four-year plan we have to submit by the end of the month. In a very real sense, administration is paid not to listen to its university visionaries. In fact, it looks at faculty, staff, and students as cogs in a fiscal wheel, elements in a shrinking economic puzzle that must be completed with fewer and fewer pieces, which ultimately is impossible. As far as I can tell, anyone who tells you to do more with less is a bad-faith actor at best. I'm simply calling it as I see it, but I can say with some rueful confidence that my views have proven to not be hyperbole, but the most measured and considered of arguments.

Still, the shit show must go on. I have a marathon in June to train for, regardless of whether it actually comes off. I may go months without a clear path into a wanton headwind that never hesitates to put me in my place. In academe especially, we get used to the idea of giving up things we hold dear, often under the guise of a "new normal." To run through a winter around here means learning how to trust one's level of fitness without always being able to hit desired paces or distances. It feels like you're going so much slower than usual, and that it takes so much extra effort to do so. Without a treadmill option, months can pass by without tempo runs or speed workouts—or even secure footing, for that matter. I can't remember the last time I completed a run completely unimpeded. Impede: from the Latin *impedire*, meaning "to shackle the feet of."

Today's doomsday prophets may indeed be the meteorologists, who are predicting wind chills of more than forty below zero come Saturday. Lonna said last night that she's already getting anxious about being able to get her run in this weekend, which is a completely endearing and runnerly response to the ultimately unknown but palpably near future. Today's weather is currently in the single digits and feels like twelve below, but the incarcerated sun has been released from isolation for its weekly hour of exercise. I hope to profit from the sunlight before it, too, goes the way of the dinosaurs. I won't run very long today, but I will do so with all the elephants and rabbits in my heart—and polar bears and pandas and wombats, oh my! I shall make of my heart an ark of teeming millions, shredding in unison.

Knife Solos

This is not a poem.	This is not a confession.	Nothing to see here.
I was afraid for my life.	I cut and I cut until	only silent oblivion
was left. Now I can no	longer fathom which	victims to honor.
I am writing this in	Boston five years after	the Boston Marathon
bombings. This is not	real news. Can an anti-	poem draw a line from
Sandy Hook to Syria?	Why do Palestinians look	at Ferguson, Missouri,
and see themselves?	Nothing to be here.	Earl says he's been
sending Mom texts	she hasn't received.	They say the storms
are now over Cleveland.	They say please watch	the marathon tomorrow
from inside. I look deep	between the lines of	the blotter sheet of my
heart and know what	five years can do to	a worldview and to
a world. Some of us know	that we lost a former	poetry student to heroin
on Monday. He was home-	less at the time he over-	dosed. They were able
to revive his girlfriend, but	not him. I read one of	my favorite poems of his
to my class on Thursday	the last line of which is	"we are no longer crouched."
I wish the same for you	you who have been caught	red-handed and full of dread
you who listen to the plain-	tive warble of an aging cat	and hear the life knell
of every future epic kitten	you who take a knee in	abject terror of the coming
weather you timorous lady-	bird beetle atop your	blade of grass, you double-
edged animal on the verge	of your most precious	discovery, you rubber-
souled visionary of our	memory care unit you	so afraid for your life
you with the weight and	heft between dust mote	and floating ash. I leave you
with every cursed thing	left to unsee and every	blessed thing left to unhear.
Now hear this: you must	run and run and run until	we are no longer crouched.

February 7, 2021

Yesterday I ran the minimum random distance I've elected to keep my newborn running streak alive—2.25 miles (RIP Ahmaud Arbery)—at a 7:21 pace. It was around -12°F, with the wind chill clocking in at -36°F. This morning my phone claims—boasts?—that it's -18°F, with that same wind chill of -36°F. So, yeah, pretty effing cold.

We knew it was coming at some point, that kind of bone-chilling cold that you want to write home about, the real ice-age deep-freeze temps Earl will mention to Mom in Michigan, perhaps to suggest that, whatever they're experiencing some 750 miles away, her son has got it worse. I suspect there's some low-grade Schadenfreude involved in his regular, some might say obsessive, comparison of temperatures throughout the land. This is a man who usually plans to spend at least part of the Michigan winter—never underestimate the nefarious strength of the proverbial Lake Effect—on a Caribbean cruise, at Hilton Head, in Key West, etc. He even took my mom to Cabbage Key one year, a mostly deserted island off the coast of Florida, no doubt with mostly poor or nonexistent reception, where they did absolutely nothing for a couple days, the normal tourist trip typically only lasting a couple hours to this bullshit historic island landmark.

In anticipation of the current ridiculous temperatures, Lonna and I stopped by Beyond Running to purchase matching blended-wool base layers, a mutual commitment to not letting our rational intuition get the best of us. I'd already proven this week that -12°F wind chill wasn't really a big deal, especially if my beautiful solar vitamin D-making machine was out and about. You might even see sporadic puddles of water basking in the sun when it's this cold. What's up with that? And though Jason, the owner of Beyond Running, told me I can always head over to their less-traveled West Fargo location to log some wind-free treadmill miles, I wanted to challenge myself to not be afraid of the bitter cold, to instill in my shredding soul what other runners seem to have known all along: you really *can* dress for the weather.

The trick lies in a combination of sensible layering and not panicking when you're out there. Tights over tights, two layers over the new base layer, hat atop the balaclava, calf-length compression socks—and underneath it all, the all-important, specially designed underwear keeping the groin area from freezing over. As Jason quipped on Thursday, you only let that happen once . . . before forty bucks for a pair of insulated briefs seems like a bargain-basement steal. I remember all too well my one time braving the elements with just a couple pairs of regular underwear underneath my tights, having to shove a glove over my junk, cupping my crotch with the other gloved hand . . . and praying.

Checking in with Mom and Michigan, as I often do on Sunday mornings while Earl is at church—which is currently being held virtually—confirms to the letter everything I've written thus far today. Earl tells Mom the forecast every morning while bemoaning the fact that winter is here for the foreseeable future. They typically get more snow than we do, but rarely have to contend with wind chills below zero. In either scenario, we all shudder to think. Lonna has just gone out after posting her intentions on social media to keep her honest, and Woodman is currently curled up in the downstairs bathroom sink for the second day in a row, soaking up the heat in the warmest room in the house. It's not supposed to get above zero around here for another long week, so by then five degrees above zero might feel rather balmy, provided the sun sticks around to brighten up the slush.

Once upon a time in the south of France, I felt the need to verify the point at which Fahrenheit and Celsius temperatures intersect. I was having a hard time explaining exactly how goddamn cold my home base was to my French family, who were used to well above-zero temps as defined by Anders Celsius. The idea of dropping below 32°F—or 0°C—was particularly unimaginable to Eliane, a lifelong proud Provençale born in Avignon.

A quick Google search confirms that the point of intersection for Fahrenheit and Celsius lies at forty degrees below zero. To live in Fargo is to know the point of intersection.

This time of year always leads me to wonder if you ever truly get used to anything. Eighteen years running (pun intended), and I still don't feel it appropriate to call Fargo–Moorhead home. Every year, there is always a day or week or month when I tell myself that I'm done with this godforsaken place, that this is the last winter Steinbeck is going to travel with Charley. I also always reach a similar breaking point in a marathon, that moment when I'm completely fine with the utterly sane idea that this will be my last 26.2 miles—or 42.2 kilometers, for my dear French family—because really, what am I doing out here? Why keep going back to the archetypal scene of the shred, that moment now over forty years ago when I ran a marathon for the first time?

Today, the Fargo question remains harder to answer than the marathon question. Something about coming into the marathon at such a tender age, with only Team Mom and a prepubescent dream in support, something about returning to the marathon fold almost thirty-three years later and having the same Mom still be there to witness it, something about the distance that encourages me to keep dreaming despite the reality of aging and general decline of civilization as we know it. Something utterly beautiful about the fact that, though we've lived apart from each other for most of our lives, Mom and I have made every effort to move through this life together, and that every marathon is an epic celebration of the excitable gift. Something elusive and ineffable in the notion that we are here to spread the word and share the love with the entire world.

I ran my PR of 2:43:42 at the Twin Cities Marathon in 2013. Circumstances dictated that I had to run it without Team Mom—and without a watch, for that matter. In addition, Lonna and her mom had just spent a week at the Mayo Clinic coming to terms with Beth's early onset dementia diagnosis, and were headed back to Fargo the day before the race. Those were fearless times for me running-wise, a period when I saw my times getting faster, when the sky was the limit for yours truly.

My last marathon—Twin Cities 2019—turned out to be my slowest, some ten minutes slower than that first marathon in Chicago at twelve years old. I knew that much had changed logistically about racing during the intervening forty years and figured that they wouldn't let Mom and me run it in together. But for some reason I got the cheeky notion to try anyway. I grabbed Mom's hands with a few hundred meters to go and said "let's see if we can jog this in." My mom—like Sexton the poet, she's Anne with an E—simply beamed. We ambled awkwardly for maybe 20 or 30 meters before a course official read me the riot act, wholly unimpressed with and unmoved by me introducing my mother to him—not like that one time at the Fiumicino airport in Italy, right, Mom? Let it be said that the race official absolutely did the right thing, while I felt both brazen and sheepish for foolishly attempting to break the rules we had all agreed to.

He couldn't possibly
know how long I've
been running with

Mom in my heart,
just as I didn't know
how simply running
20 or 30 meters on
course hand-in-hand
with Anne Brandt
would be more than
enough. Or that it
would last a lifetime.

Acknowledgments

"Object Trajectory" & "Wilma" *Chattahoochee Review*
"American Childhood" *Unbound: Composing Home*, New Rivers Press 2022
"Purr" *Thin Air*
"Beatlemania" *The New Guard* (Editor's Edition, Volume X)

Thank you!

To everyone at NDSU Press—in particular Sarah Beck, Suzzanne Kelley & Nayt Rundquist—for believing in the manuscript and turning it into a book with legs. You all shred.

To Anne Brandt, Fred Schmalz, Michael Tomanek & Lonna Whiting, for reading early versions of the manuscript and making it way better.

To my erstwhile New Rivers Press comrades Tara Ballard and Elizabeth Searle, for your kind words, and for getting it.

To the Beyond Running community, for running and being there—come rain, sleet, snow, seasonal affective disorder, pandemic, climate catastrophe, etc.

To the students at MSUM who believe in the idea of reading and writing toward a better world. May we cross paths again before too long.

To those who make Fargo–Moorhead the place to be, including: Beyond Running, Ecumen at the Evergreens, Elemental Running Club, Fargo Brewing Company, Faster Stronger Runner, Harold's, Junkyard Brewing, Lake Agassiz Pacers, my colleagues at MSUM, NDSU Press, Orange Records, Sammy's Pizza, Silver Lining Creamery, Swing Barrel, Thunder Coffee & Zandbroz Variety.

And to you, for sharing the page with me.

—Peace & justice, KC

In loving memory: Brittney Goodman
Elizabeth Gregory
Amos Tevelow
Gracie

About the Author

Kevin Carollo has taught world literature and writing at Minnesota State University Moorhead for twenty years. He received his doctorate in comparative literature from the University of Illinois—Urbana-Champaign and is author of *Elizabeth Gregory* (Rain Taxi/OHM Editions), a poetry chapbook about early onset dementia. His poems have appeared in *Collateral, Conduit, Cream City Review, Ellipsis, Little Patuxent Review, Moon City Review, The New Guard, RHINO, Thin Air,* and elsewhere. He ran his first marathon shortly after turning twelve years old. Since 2014, he has completed the Boston Marathon seven times. He lives, writes, and runs in Fargo, North Dakota.

About NDSU Press

North Dakota State University Press (NDSU Press) exists to stimulate and coordinate interdisciplinary regional scholarship. These regions include the Red River Valley, the state of North Dakota, the plains of North America (comprising both the Great Plains of the United States and the prairies of Canada), and comparable regions of other continents. We publish peer reviewed regional scholarship shaped by national and international events and comparative studies.

Neither topic nor discipline limits the scope of NDSU Press publications. We consider manuscripts in any field of learning. We define our scope, however, by a regional focus in accord with the press's mission. Generally, works published by NDSU Press address regional life directly, as the subject of study. Such works contribute to scholarly knowledge of region (that is, discovery of new knowledge) or to public consciousness of region (that is, dissemination of information or interpretation of regional experience). Where regions abroad are treated, either for comparison or because of ties to those North American regions of primary concern to the press, the linkages are made plain. For nearly three-quarters of a century, NDSU Press has published substantial trade books, but the line of publications is not limited to that genre. We also publish textbooks (at any level), reference books, anthologies, reprints, papers, proceedings, and monographs. The press also considers works of poetry or fiction, provided they are established regional classics or they promise to assume landmark or reference status for the region. We select biographical or autobiographical works carefully for their prospective contribution to regional knowledge and culture. All publications, in whatever genre, are of such quality and substance as to embellish the imprint of NDSU Press.

Our name changed to North Dakota State University Press in January 2016. Prior to that, and since 1950, we published as the North Dakota Institute for Regional Studies Press. We continue to operate under the umbrella of the North Dakota Institute for Regional Studies, located at North Dakota State University.